Of the People

An African American Cooking Experience

Dedicated

to Dr. Charles H. Wright and the ancestors

Published by the Charles H. Wright Museum of African American History

Copyright © Charles H. Wright Museum of African American History
315 East Warren Avenue, Detroit, Michigan 48201

Executive Editors: Dawn Foster Langford, Damaris Hill

Contributing Editor: Coraleen Rawls

Photographers: Robert Vigeletti, Felecia Hunt-Taylor

Designed, edited, and manufactured in the United States of America
by Favorite Recipes® Press, an imprint of

FRP™

2451 Atrium Way, Nashville, Tennessee 37214
1-800-358-0560

Book Design: Steve Newman
Managing Editor: Mary Cummings
Project Manager: Jane Hinshaw
Production Manager: Mark Sloan
Project Production: Sara Anglin

Library of Congress Number: 99-070172
ISBN: 0-9667873-0-7
First Printing: 1999   7,500

Contents

Foreword

Kimberly Camp
Former President of the MAAH

It gives me great pleasure to present *Of the People: An African American Cooking Experience*. This book is a wonderful opportunity for the Museum of African American History to celebrate our mission in a way that is educational and fun for all of us—in celebrating our culinary traditions.

The Museum is dedicated to the preservation, documentation, and education of the public on the history, life, and culture of African Americans. We serve as a resource center for the enhancement on knowledge and understanding about African Americans. Whether it is our experiences in the rural South, our migrations to the industrialized North, or our origins on the continent of Africa, our rich cultural heritage continues to grow. Ours is a story that has been little told and little understood. Our food ways are central to that experience and contain the traditions and practices of our ancestors.

The recipes contained in this book are a celebration of the breadth of our experiences. Our African origins gave us foods that are central in our culinary practices. Okra, yams, sesame seeds, and many other foods originate on the continent of Africa and were brought here during the Transatlantic Slave trade. Where traditional African foods could not be found, we improvised with indigenous fruits and vegetables. The tradition of using spices, including our love of "hot" foods, can also be traced to our African roots.

Still other traditions were born from the African diaspora, with contributions to our food ways from central and south America, the Caribbean, United States of America, and Canada. The slight differences in the way we make our sweet potato pies, cook our collard greens, or make fried apple pies give us hints to our ancestry and ethnicity with the African American community.

My family is a typical example of the range of culinary traditions we all share. Some evenings, when I convince my husband Seydou to cook, he will whip up a mean groundnut stew with peanut butter, chicken, and okra over rice. At family reunions, it is Uncle Donald's elderberry dumplings and homemade ice cream that we all line up for after a good helping of Uncle Jim's barbecue and his own special sauce. My father can make an awesome oyster stew, even though he hails from the mountains of Pennsylvania and my Grandpa Early Dimery would make sweet potato bread that was even better than grandma's. Still, my mother's roast beef and pound cake would always signal a special occasion as the smells of both would waft from the kitchen stove.

To create this book, we asked people in our community to share their recipes, all of which have been taste tested and believe me—you are in for a treat. This book is a great addition to any chef's library, and makes a great gift for newlyweds, college grads or yourself! The proceeds from its sale allow the Museum to continue to provide quality programs and exhibitions for all. Enjoy!

Introduction

Margaret Thomas-Ward
Archivist

The Charles H. Wright Museum of African American History in Detroit, Michigan has developed in three major phases. It has grown from its idealistic beginnings in 1965 to its emergence as a sophisticated world-class Museum in 1997. The name changes mark the Museum's evolution and corporate identities: The International Afro-American Museum (IAM) 1965; Afro-American Museum of Detroit (AAM) 1975; Museum of African American History (MAAH) 1987; and currently the Charles H. Wright Museum of African American History 1998. The different periods allowed the Museum to evolve into a world-class cultural icon in the Detroit Cultural Center.

In the beginning, Dr. Charles H. Wright, a prominent Detroit obstetrician, attended a medical convention in Denmark. There, he visited a memorial to Danish World War II heroes. This experience inspired him with the idea of creating a museum to honor African Americans. With charismatic zeal, Dr. Wright enlisted the support of the community in implementing his dream.

The International Afro-American Museum (IAM) was founded in 1965. On March 10, 1965, Dr. Wright and a racially integrated group of 33 Detroit citizens met to consider a proposal to establish a museum dedicated to Black history. The primary goal of the project was to strengthen the self image of Blacks by directly involving the Black Community in the creation of the museum, and providing historically documented information. A museum of this kind was intended to foster a sense of pride in Black Americans' past and a belief in their potential for future accomplishments.

The International Afro-American Museum opened its doors for the first time on January 30, 1966, at 1549 W. Grand Boulevard in a building owned by Dr. Wright. It was funded by memberships, donations, and financial support provided by Detroit area churches and social and civic institutions. The Museum's first exhibition went on display at the University of Detroit during the National Conference of Educators in late 1966. Also during this same year, the Museum acquired a non-profit charter.

In these founding years, the Museum grew rapidly, soon occupying three adjoining buildings on the corner of West Grand and Warren avenues. It remained at this location for 20 years. During the West Grand Boulevard years, the Museum produced many exhibitions touching on various aspects of Black culture, arts of Africa, the role of Blacks in the American Revolution, The Underground Railroad, the Montgomery boycott, Rosa Parks, and the life and work of Paul Robeson. A "Museum on Wheels," the mobile Museum, was created when a mobile home was purchased in 1967 as an outreach project to schools, churches, and public locations. The conversion of the mobile home into a mini-traveling museum, operated by volunteers, opened its first exhibition at the 1967 Michigan State Fair shortly after the 1967 Riot.

In the 1970s, the energy engendered by grass-roots spirit and community support resulted in the Museum's producing a number of projects such as *Spotlight On Black America*, a weekly broadcast on WCHB radio and two films: *You Can be a Doctor* and *The Bank Is Open To You*. The Museum was also instrumental in the publication of two books: *Blacks In The Age of The American Revolution*, by Colin Palmer, and *Robeson: Labor's Forgotten Champion*, by Dr. Charles H. Wright.

The Museum frequently exhibited the works of local Black artists. Two murals by noted Detroit artist Leroy Foster were commissioned by the Museum. *The Life and Times of Frederick Douglass*, a joint venture with the Detroit Public Library, was unveiled in 1972 at the Library's Frederick Douglass Branch. The second mural, *Kaleidoscope*, was unveiled at Southwest Detroit Hospital, as a joint venture between the Museum, medical staff, and hospital administration.

As the Museum's collections and audiences grew, so did the need for a new building. The expansion years began when in 1975, the Board of Trustees of the International Afro-American Museum (IAM), changed the name to The Afro-American Museum of Detroit (AAM).

On September 11, 1978, the City of Detroit agreed to lease the property on Frederick, between John R and Brush streets in the Cultural Center, for the site of a new museum. In June 1979, a Building Fund Campaign was launched. To raise the necessary funds to build, furnish, and equip the new Museum, as well as to expand the collection and generate ongoing operational support, "funding campaigns" became the focus of the 80s. Mayor Coleman A. Young committed $2.3 million dollars in block grant funds for the construction of the new museum. Interest and support for the Museum and contributions in the Building Fund Campaign came from across the State of Michigan. In 1981, a Buy-A-Brick Campaign began to allow community organizations, clubs, businesses, churches, and public schools to play an active role as contributors. In 1983, the Museum launched a Million Dollar Club membership recruitment drive, which entitled supporters to a life-long membership and special benefits through a $1,000 or more contribution. At the same time, exciting annual events, which marked the decade, attracted the community and raised funds for Museum programs. The Jim Ramsey Street Race and Fun Walk, a 10K(6.2 miles) race and two-mile fun walk, thrilled participants and cheering crowds. The Museum presented its first African World Festival, entitled *The African World Is One*.

On May 21, 1985 Mayor Coleman A. Young and Dr. Wright led groundbreaking ceremonies for the new building in the Cultural Center. The building was designed by Detroit architectural firm, Sims-Varner and Associates. On May 8, 1987, throngs of jubilant Detroiters and other visitors, led by Dr. Wright and Mayor Young, marched from the Rackham Building on Farnsworth Street to the ribbon cutting at the entrance of the new building at 301 Frederick Douglass Street. Symbolically, the name of Frederick Street where the new Museum edifice was located was changed to Frederick Douglass, named for the famous African American abolitionist. The Inaugural Day scene created a powerful image. A beautiful triangular building crowned by geometric cones, reminiscent of Dogon huts (a structure used to build homes by the Dogon African people), welcomed the world to the Museum of African American History (MAAH). The inaugural exhibit, *An Epic of Heroism: The Underground Railroad in Michigan, 1837-1870*, depicted information collected by African American scholars. In June of the inaugural year, the Louise Lovett Wright Library was dedicated to serve as an informational center and archive not only for the Museum, but for the scholarly community at large.

The metamorphosis, from three row houses to a new building in the Cultural Center, opened a new era. MAAH became at once a community gathering place where all forums were welcomed and new traditions established. A quarterly publication, *African American News*, became the Museum's official newsletter. Kwanzaa became a week-long celebration. The African World Festival, held on Detroit's riverfront Hart Plaza, became a hallmark of the Museum. The Festival celebrates the African diaspora and attracts vendors from all over the world to sell their wares and crafts to the thousands of people who attend.

By the 1990s, the winds of change touched Detroit and the Museum. When Nelson Mandela visited Detroit that year, the Museum became an integral part of the City's celebration of his freedom. Soon, MAAH became a part of a new master plan which had emerged from a proposal by the University Cultural Center Association and the City of Detroit. MAAH's trustees accepted the opportunity to move with the currents which would allow the Museum to expand its facilities and further the goals of the Museum to educate and inspire all people. Planning for the present building began in 1990.

Detroit voters passed a proposal in 1992, giving the City of Detroit authority to sell bonds to construct a third generation Museum of African American History. August, 1993 marked the groundbreaking ceremonies for the new Museum of African American History. With the support of Mayor Dennis Archer in 1996, the Museum campaigned for an additional 10 million dollar bond to complete the construction of the new MAAH edifice. In August, 1996, Detroit voters overwhelmingly voted approval of the proposal.

"Jubilation: Celebrating The Spirit" was the theme in April of 1997 at the Grand Opening of the Museum of African American History's world-class landmark structure located at 315 E. Warren in the Cultural Center. Festivities for the opening began with media previews and a red carpet black-tie gala benefit. On Saturday, April 12, Mayor Dennis Archer, along with other dignitaries, led the ribbon cutting and dedication ceremony.

The world's largest Museum of African American History features three exhibitions galleries, a theater, classrooms, an archive and research library, a store, and a restaurant. Mounted above the main entrance doors are two African masks designed by Detroit artist Richard Bennett. Underneath the spectacular rotunda glass dome, is an equally impressive floor with a mosaic mural designed by Detroit artist Hubert Massey. The mural, called *Genealogy*, is the artist's interpretation of the struggle endured by African Americans in this country.

The core exhibit in the Museum's 120,000 square foot building is entitled, *Of the People: The African American Experience*. Major themes which are recounted in the African American Experience begin with "The African Memory" and continue with "The Crime; Survival of the Spirit;" "The Imperfect Union; Freedom and Betrayal;" "Urban Struggle for Empowerment;" and "Becoming of the Future." The Museum also has two changing exhibition galleries which host traveling exhibitions that feature various aspects of the African and African American culture. Because of its mission, its exhibits, and its unique architecture, the Museum attracts visitors and dignitaries from all over the U.S. and the world.

As a tribute to the founder, Dr. Charles H. Wright, the Board of Trustees of the Museum and the Detroit City Council announced on March 30, 1998 that the name of the Museum of African American History was officially changed to the Charles H. Wright Museum of African American History.

To further continue the Museum's mission, the Museum has embarked on the creation of new exhibition projects, which will be made available for travel to other institutions following their opening at the CHWMAAH. One of the exhibitions scheduled to travel is *Land of Promise: Detroit's Black Bottom and Paradise Valley*. We welcome your visit and encourage your membership.

Mission Statement

The Charles H. Wright Museum of African American History documents, preserves and educates the public on the history, life and culture of African Americans. The Museum serves as the resource center for the enhancement of knowledge and understanding about African Americans.

Special Recipe Contributors

Wendell Anthony
Bishop P. A. Brooks
C. David Campbell
Sheila M. Cockrel
Julius V. Combs
Robert N. Cooper
Camille O. Cosby

George F. Francis, III
Ana Gabriel
Ronald E. Goldsberry
Earl G. Graves
William T. Johnson
Celeste Stokes McDermott
Shirley F. Moulton

Juliette Okotie-Eboh
Earnestine Oliver
Nettie Seabrooks
Judith Sims
Janet Tinsley
Merle Mitchell Watts
Weight Watchers

NKONSONKONSON

(corn-song-corn-song)

The African symbol NKONSONKONSON is the symbol of the chain or link of human relations in which the interdependence of each person, or link, determines the success of the community, or chain. It reflects the links with the past and the hope for strength through cooperation in the future.

...when the history books are written in future generations the historians will have to pause and say, 'There lived a great people—a black people—who injected new meaning and dignity into the veins of civilization.' —Martin Luther King, Jr.

The memories of the past are important as they define the significance of the present. Celebrations of that past are always centered around the food that is representative of it and the memories evoked by it.

African cooking is highly diverse because of the various cultures and climates from which it originates, but it also has similarities based on the available ingredients common to all the cultures and the limited means of food preservation. In all cases, however, African food is served with a spirit of hospitality and celebration and brings the same spirit to the meal wherever it is served around the world today.

Africa
The African Memory

SANKƆFA
(sang-ko-fah)

Go back and fetch it

SANKƆFA is the symbol of the wisdom of learning
from the past to build for the future.

Chinchin
Sweet Dough Balls

1 cup self-rising flour   *Nigeria*
1 cup flour
1 teaspoon baking powder
$^1/_2$ cup sugar, or to taste
1 teaspoon grated nutmeg
2 teaspoons dry yeast
$^1/_2$ to $^3/_4$ cup water
food coloring (optional)
vegetable oil for deep-frying

Sift the self-rising flour, flour and baking powder together in a large bowl. Stir in the sugar, nutmeg and yeast.

Heat the water and food coloring to 130 degrees in a saucepan. Add to the flour mixture gradually, mixing to form a soft dough. Let rise, covered, in a warm place for 1 hour.

Shape into small balls. Deep-fry in the heated oil in a skillet until the outside browns. Reduce the heat and fry until the center is cooked through, turning to cook evenly. Drain on paper towels.

Serve as an appetizer or as a treat at festive occasions.

For a richer dough, add milk and eggs.

Serves four to six

Esstata
Plantain Appetizer

10 large ripe plantains or bananas
½ cup sour milk
3 eggs
½ cup butter
pinch of salt
16 ounces corn flour

Mash the plantains in a large bowl. Add the milk, eggs, butter and salt. Mix well with a wooden spoon or rotary beater. Add the corn flour and mix to form a soft dough.

Place in a greased heat-proof bowl and cover with foil, sealing well. Place the bowl in a larger saucepan or steamer containing hot water; cover tightly. Steam for 1½ hours.

Serve hot with stewed mushrooms, other vegetables or stews. Refrigerate leftovers and slice. Fry in oil or reheat in the oven.

Serves twenty

If you understand the beginning well, the end will not trouble you. —Ashanti proverb

Groundnut Soup
Peanut Soup

1 (4- to 6-pound) chicken, cut up   *Ghana*
2 medium onions, chopped
vegetable oil
salt to taste
4 medium tomatoes
1 pound groundnut paste or 1¾ cups peanut butter
12 cups water
2 fresh red peppers or ground red pepper to taste

Cook the chicken with the onions in oil in a large saucepan until golden brown. Season with salt to taste. Add the tomatoes and just enough cold water to cover the chicken. Bring to a boil and reduce the heat. Simmer for 15 minutes.

Remove the tomatoes from the soup. Scoop the pulp from the tomatoes and add it to the chicken mixture, discarding the skins. Blend the groundnut paste with a small amount of hot cooking liquid in a bowl and stir it into the soup. Add 12 cups of water and the red peppers. Cook over low heat until the oil rises to the top.

Remove the chicken from the soup if necessary to prevent it from overcooking, and return it to the saucepan to serve.

Serves six

Tomato Soup

1 small onion, finely chopped   *South Africa*
1 small carrot, finely chopped
2 tablespoons vegetable oil or shortening
2 tablespoons flour
4 cups hot water
4 medium tomatoes, chopped
1 teaspoon sugar
salt and pepper to taste

Sauté the onion and carrot in the oil in a saucepan. Cover the saucepan and reduce the heat. Steam for 10 minutes.

Stir in the flour until smooth. Add the hot water, tomatoes, sugar, salt and pepper. Simmer for 10 minutes longer.

Serves four

Treat the world well....It was not given to you by your parents....It was willed to you by your children.
—Kenyan proverb

Raita
Cucumber and Yogurt Salad

2 large cucumbers   South Africa
yogurt
$1/2$ to 1 teaspoon cumin seeds
$1/2$ to 1 teaspoon finely chopped fresh mint (optional)

Grate or slice the cucumbers and measure the amount. Combine with an equal amount of yogurt in a bowl and mix well.

Toast the cumin seeds in a hot cast-iron skillet until brown, stirring constantly. Pound the toasted seeds and stir into the cucumber mixture. Stir in the mint.

Chill until serving time. Serve with curries.

Serves four to six

Rooibeet Slaai
Red Beet Salad

4 medium beets, cooked, chopped
1 small onion, finely chopped
$1/2$ teaspoon sugar
$1/2$ teaspoon salt
1 to 2 tablespoons vinegar

South Africa

Combine the beets and onion in a bowl and mix well. Combine the sugar, salt and vinegar in a bowl and stir until sugar and salt are dissolved. Pour over the beet mixture and mix well.
Chill until serving time.

Serves four to six

If you don't remember where you came from or how you got from there to here, you have a very hard time moving on. And you have to have goals to move from where you are. —Ada Deblanc Simonel

Dodo
Steak Supreme with Corn Flour Balls

1 pound rump steak   Kenya
2 tablespoons vegetable oil or shortening
1 cup water
1 tomato, peeled, chopped
1/4 teaspoon baking soda
salt to taste
1/2 cup peanut butter
1/2 cup water
1 tomato, sliced
Sima

Cut the steak into 4 pieces. Brown in the heated oil in a skillet. Add 1 cup of water, the chopped tomato, baking soda and salt. Simmer until the liquid is reduced to 1/2 cup.

Blend the peanut butter with 1/2 cup of water in a bowl. Add to the skillet. Simmer until the steak is tender and the sauce is thickened.

Arrange the steak on a serving platter and spoon the sauce over the top. Top with the sliced tomato. Serve with Sima.

Sima

2 cups water
1 1/2 cups corn flour
1 tablespoon butter
1 egg
milk

Bring the water to a boil in a saucepan. Stir the flour gradually into the water with a wooden spoon. Cook over low heat until thickened. Add the butter. Cook for 10 minutes longer or until the outside forms a transparent film, stirring constantly. Shape by spoonfuls into balls. Whisk the egg and a small amount of milk together in a bowl. Dip the dough balls into the egg mixture. Brown in the oven, or broil for 2 to 3 minutes until brown.

Serves four

Jollof Rice

1 pound lean beef or chicken 　　　　　　　　　　　*Mali*
salt and white pepper to taste
vegetable oil for browning the beef
3½ cups stock, or water with 3 crushed bouillon cubes
3 large onions, finely chopped
4 garlic cloves, minced
2 or 3 chiles, finely chopped
4 large tomatoes, blanched, peeled, mashed
3 tablespoons tomato paste
8 ounces carrots, green beans, mushrooms,
*   bell peppers or vegetables of choice*
1 pound uncooked long grain rice

Cut the beef into 2-inch cubes and sprinkle with salt and pepper. Let stand, covered, for 1 to 2 hours. Brown the beef in hot oil in a skillet. Drain the skillet, reserving a small amount of the oil in the skillet.

Add the beef to the stock in a large saucepan. Simmer until the beef begins to become tender. Remove from the heat.

Sauté the onions, garlic and chiles in the reserved oil in the skillet. Stir in the tomatoes, tomato paste, half the chopped vegetables and 1 cup of stock from the beef mixture and mix well. Simmer for 5 to 7 minutes.

Add to meat mixture. Stir in the rice. Simmer, covered, for 15 minutes. Arrange the remaining chopped vegetables on top of the rice. Simmer until the meat and rice are tender and all the stock is absorbed, adding additional water in small amounts if necessary. Top servings with chopped lettuce, parsley or cilantro and hard-cooked eggs.

Serves four to six

Varenga
Shredded Chuck

2 pounds boneless chuck beef   *Malagasy Republic*
2 tablespoons salt
1 garlic clove
1 onion, sliced

Cut the beef into small pieces. Combine with the salt, garlic and onion in a 2-quart saucepan. Add enough water to cover the beef. Bring to a boil and reduce the heat.

Simmer, covered, for 2 hours or until the beef is tender enough to shred with a fork, adding additional water if needed. Strain the broth and shred the beef.

Place the beef in a 7x11-inch baking dish. Bake at 400 degrees for 30 minutes or until meat is browned.

Serves six

It's up to the living to keep in touch with the ancestors.
—Julie Dash, *Daughters of the Dust*

Tamale Pie

8 ounces ground meat (preferably some pork)   Kenya
3 garlic cloves, minced
1 medium onion, chopped
2½ cups canned tomatoes, or 6 ounces tomato sauce
1 teaspoon salt
1 teaspoon sugar
2 tablespoons chili powder, or oregano, marjoram
   and cumin to taste
1 cup water
1 cup cornmeal
1½ teaspoons salt
1 (8-ounce) can whole kernel corn, drained
½ cup sliced black olives
1 (10-ounce) can pinto or kidney beans, rinsed, drained
½ cup shredded Cheddar cheese

Combine the ground meat, garlic, onion, tomatoes, salt, sugar and chili powder in a bowl and mix well.

Combine the water, cornmeal and salt in a saucepan and mix well. Cook over medium heat until thickened, stirring constantly. Press over the bottom and sides of a 9x13-inch baking dish.

Layer half the meat mixture, the corn, olives, pinto beans and remaining meat mixture in the prepared dish. Sprinkle with the cheese. Bake at 350 degrees for 40 minutes or until cooked through.

Serves six

Bamia
Okra and Lamb Stew

3 onions, finely chopped   *Egypt*
4 garlic cloves, chopped
6 tablespoons vegetable oil or samna
    (Egyptian rich clarified butter)
3 pounds lamb, cubed
salt and pepper to taste
2 pounds fresh okra, trimmed, sliced 1/4 inch thick
2 teaspoons tomato paste
1 cup water
8 ounces tomatoes, blanched, peeled, chopped
1 sprig fresh cilantro
juice of 1 lemon (optional)

Cook the onions and garlic in the oil in a heavy saucepan until they begin to brown. Add the lamb and season with salt and pepper. Cook until the lamb begins to brown. Stir in the okra. Cook over low heat for 10 to 15 minutes or until the okra is tender-crisp.

Blend the tomato paste with the water in a cup. Add to the saucepan with the tomatoes and mix well. Adjust the seasoning.

Simmer for 40 minutes or until the lamb and vegetables are tender and the sauce is thickened to the desired consistency, adding additional water if needed. Stir in the cilantro and lemon juice. Serve hot with rice or couscous.

Veal or beef may be substituted for the more traditional lamb in this dish.

Serves four

Lamb with Couscous

Tunisia

4 pounds lamb, cut up
3 to 4 large onions, chopped
1/2 cup olive oil
1 (6-ounce) can tomato paste
2 cups chopped fresh tomatoes
2 green bell peppers, coarsely chopped
5 garlic cloves, chopped
1 tablespoon ground cumin
1 teaspoon curry powder
1 teaspoon cayenne pepper
1 teaspoon black pepper
salt to taste
1 large butternut squash, peeled, seeded, chopped
4 medium turnips, coarsely chopped
4 carrots, sliced
1 pound onions, finely chopped
1 pound potatoes, chopped
2 cups uncooked couscous, cooked
2 green onions, chopped
3 sprigs of parsley, chopped
1 to 2 lemons, cut into wedges

Brown the lamb and the 3 to 4 large onions in the olive oil in a large saucepan. Stir in the tomato paste. Cook for 5 minutes, stirring frequently.

Add the tomatoes, green peppers, garlic, cumin, curry powder, cayenne pepper, black pepper and salt; mix well. Simmer for 15 minutes.

Add the squash, turnips, carrots, the finely chopped onions and potatoes. Add enough water to come within 3 inches of the top of the mixture. Simmer until the lamb and vegetables are tender.

Spoon the couscous onto serving plates. Spoon the lamb mixture over the couscous. Top with green onions, parsley and lemon wedges.

Serves six to eight

Basic Curry

½ cup chopped onion   *Somalia*
3 tablespoons vegetable oil
3 tablespoons flour
2 teaspoons ground cumin
½ teaspoon ground ginger
1½ teaspoons coriander
½ teaspoon turmeric
¼ teaspoon ground cloves
½ teaspoon cinnamon
2 teaspoons curry powder
1 teaspoon salt
¼ teaspoon red pepper
1 teaspoon black pepper
lemon juice and grated lemon peel to taste
2 cups liquid
2 cups chopped cooked meat, fish or vegetables

Brown the onion in the heated oil in a skillet. Mix the flour, cumin, ginger, coriander, turmeric, cloves, cinnamon, curry powder, salt, red pepper and black pepper together. Add to the onion. Cook over low heat for 3 minutes, stirring constantly.

Stir in the lemon juice, lemon peel and liquid. Simmer until liquid is of the desired consistency. Stir in the meat, fish or vegetables. Cook until heated through. Serve meat or fish curry with rice; serve vegetable curry with meat.

For the liquid in this dish, use stock or chicken broth. Coconut milk is delicious with shrimp curry. All curry dishes are better on the second day.

Serves six

Berberé
Spice Mixture

Ethiopia and Eritrea

1 tablespoon paprika
1 to 3 teaspoons cayenne pepper
1 teaspoon garlic powder
1 tablespoon ground ginger
1 teaspoon dried savory, crushed
1 teaspoon dried basil, crushed
1½ teaspoons ground cumin
½ teaspoon ground turmeric
½ teaspoon ground allspice
¼ teaspoon ground cinnamon
1 teaspoon dry mustard
1½ teaspoons ground coriander
½ teaspoon ground cloves
½ teaspoon salt

Combine the paprika, cayenne pepper, garlic powder, ginger, savory, basil, cumin, turmeric, allspice, cinnamon, mustard, coriander, cloves and salt in a bowl and mix well. Store in a jar with a tight-fitting lid for up to 2 months. Use in soups and stews.

Makes one-fourth cup

Chicken and Sauce

1 (4- to 6-pound) chicken, cut up   *Mali*
salt and pepper to taste
1 large onion, chopped
1/2 cup vegetable oil or shortening
2 tomatoes, peeled, chopped
1 1/2 tablespoons tomato paste
4 cups water
1/2 head cabbage
chopped eggplant
2 carrots, sliced
5 small fresh okra pods
1 small bay leaf
1 tablespoon corn or wheat flour

Sprinkle the chicken with salt and pepper. Cook the chicken with the onion in the heated oil in a skillet over medium heat until browned on all sides.

Add the tomatoes, tomato paste and 4 cups water. Bring to a boil. Add the cabbage, eggplant, carrots, okra and bay leaf. Simmer for 1 to 1 1/2 hours or until the chicken is cooked through.

Whisk the flour with a small amount of water in a bowl. Stir into the chicken mixture. Cook until of the desired consistency. Discard bay leaf. Serve with rice.

Serves four or five

Maafe
Chicken and Groundnut Stew

1 chicken, cut up   Mali
salt to taste
3 medium onions, finely chopped
groundnut (peanut) oil for browning the chicken
2 tablespoons tomato paste
1/4 cup water
2 red chiles, finely chopped
4 medium tomatoes, blanched, peeled, chopped
1 cup smooth groundnut (peanut) paste
2 1/4 cups boiling water
8 okra pods, trimmed
2 sweet potatoes or yams, peeled, cubed
8 ounces corn kernels
4 carrots, cut into 4 to 6 pieces
turnips or other firm root vegetable
cinnamon and paprika to taste

Season the chicken with salt. Cook the chicken with the onions in the heated oil in a Dutch oven until the chicken is brown.

Blend the tomato paste with 1/4 cup water in a small bowl. Stir into the chicken. Add the chiles and tomatoes. Whisk the groundnut paste into the boiling water until smooth. Stir into the chicken mixture.

Simmer for 40 minutes, stirring occasionally. Add the okra, sweet potatoes, corn, carrots, turnips, cinnamon, paprika and salt. Simmer until the chicken is cooked through and the sauce is of the desired consistency. Serve with rice, potato croquettes or cooked root vegetables.

Serves four

Djaj M'Kalli
Chicken with Lemons and Olives

3 chickens
6 garlic cloves, crushed
2 tablespoons salt
¾ cup vegetable oil
2 teaspoons ginger
1 teaspoon turmeric
1 teaspoon pepper
saffron and salt to taste
3 medium onions, grated
½ cup butter
2 garlic cloves, chopped
1 quart water
3 ounces kalamata olives
2 pickled lemons, rinsed

Morocco

Trim the fat from the chickens. Rub with a mixture of 6 garlic cloves and 2 tablespoons salt. Place in a large bowl and add enough water to cover. Let stand in the refrigerator for 1 hour.

Mix the oil, ginger, turmeric, pepper, saffron and salt to taste in a bowl for the marinade. Drain the chickens and pat dry. Rub with the oil mixture. Marinate in the refrigerator for several hours.

Combine the chickens, onions, butter, 2 garlic cloves and 1 quart water in a large saucepan. Bring to a boil and reduce the heat. Simmer until the chickens are tender, adding the olives and pickled lemons when almost tender. Remove the chickens to a platter. Boil the cooking liquid until thickened. Return the chickens to the saucepan and reheat to serve.

To pickle lemons, cut lemons into quarters, cutting to, but not through, the stem end. Fill with salt and pack into an airtight jar. Let stand for 2 weeks or longer.

Serves eight

Fish Cakes

¼ cup flour or bread crumbs   Lesotho
1 egg
¼ cup water or milk
8 ounces fish fillets
salt and pepper to taste
1 medium onion, chopped
2 tablespoons vegetable oil or shortening

Combine the flour, egg and water in a bowl and mix until smooth. Cut the fish into small pieces. Stir the fish, salt, pepper and onion into the flour mixture.

Heat the oil in a skillet. Drop the fish mixture by spoonfuls into the hot oil. Cook until browned on all sides.

Serves two

Ancestors, Ancestors guide me to whatever I'm looking for, whatever it may be. —Ethiopian proverb

Tiébou Dienn
Fish Stew

2 bunches fresh parsley   Senegal
2 large yellow onions
2 or 3 green onions
4 to 6 garlic cloves
2 tablespoons soy sauce
1 teaspoon salt
1 tablespoon (heaping) pepper
1 (3- to 4-pound) thick white fish
vegetable oil for frying
2 or 3 onions, finely chopped
3 tablespoons soy sauce
4 ounces tomato paste
6 cups water
4 each carrots and turnips, peeled
1 small cabbage
2 eggplant
5 sweet potatoes, peeled
6 to 8 okra pods
1 chile pepper, or to taste, or cayenne pepper to taste
3 cups uncooked rice

Combine the first 7 ingredients in a blender or food processor container. Process until smooth. Cut deep pockets in the fish, taking care not to cut all the way through. Stuff the parsley purée into the fish. Heat 2 to 3 inches of oil in a large heavy saucepan. Add the fish and fry until golden brown; remove and drain the fish.

Pour off all but 2 tablespoons of the oil. Add 2 or 3 chopped onions, 3 tablespoons soy sauce, tomato paste and water and mix well. Cut the carrots, turnips, cabbage, eggplant and sweet potatoes into large chunks. Add to the saucepan with the okra and chile pepper. Cook over medium heat until the vegetables are tender, adding the fish toward the end of the cooking time.

Remove the fish and vegetables to a dish; keep warm. Add enough water to the liquid in the saucepan to measure 6 cups. Add the rice and cook until tender. Spread the rice in a large bowl. Top with the fish and vegetables.

Serves six to ten

Yassa Au Poisson
Marinated Fish

1/2 large red pepper, sliced   *Senegal*
juice of 2 lemons, about 1/2 cup
2 tablespoons vinegar
1/2 teaspoon salt
1/4 teaspoon black pepper
1/2 cup palm oil
3 small fresh gilt-heads or mullets
4 small onions, sliced
1 1/2 cups water

Combine the red pepper, lemon juice, vinegar, salt, black pepper and a few drops of the oil in a bowl and mix well.

Heat 1/4 cup of the remaining oil in a skillet until very hot. Add the fish and cook until brown.

Heat the remaining oil in a second skillet. Add the onions and cook until brown. Add the pepper mixture, grilled fish and water. Simmer, covered, for 10 minutes. Serve with white rice.

Serves five

Atakelte
Braised Cabbage

$^1/_2$ head green cabbage, shredded   *Ethiopia*
1 yellow onion, chopped
2 to 3 tablespoons vegetable oil
1 cup tomato sauce
2 carrots, peeled, chopped
2 potatoes, peeled, chopped (optional)
$^1/_2$ cup water
salt to taste
cayenne pepper or other ground red chile pepper
      to taste (optional)

Cook the cabbage in a small amount of water in a saucepan over medium heat for 5 minutes or until tender, stirring frequently. Cook the onion in a small amount of water in a skillet over medium-high heat for 5 minutes or until the water evaporates. Reduce the heat to medium and stir in the oil. Cook until the onion begins to brown. Add the tomato sauce, carrots, potatoes and $^1/_2$ cup of water.

Simmer for 10 to 15 minutes. Add the cabbage, salt and cayenne pepper and mix well. Simmer, covered, for 10 minutes longer.

Serves six

Stuffed Eggplant

Ghana

1 large eggplant
salt to taste
1 small onion, chopped
2 tablespoons vegetable oil
1/4 cup bread crumbs
2 tablespoons grated Parmesan cheese
1 teaspoon oregano
1 teaspoon salt
pepper to taste
1 egg, slightly beaten

Cook the eggplant in enough boiling salted water to cover in a saucepan for 30 minutes or until tender but still firm. Remove the eggplant from the water and cool. Cut into halves lengthwise and scoop out the pulp, reserving the shells.

Sauté the onion in the oil in a skillet until tender. Add the eggplant pulp and mash together with a fork. Stir in the bread crumbs, cheese, oregano, 1 teaspoon salt, pepper and egg. Spoon the mixture into the reserved eggplant shells. Place in a baking dish. Bake at 350 degrees for 30 minutes. Serve with beef.

Serves six

Kelewele
Spicy Fried Plantain

2 teaspoons ground ginger   Ghana
1/2 teaspoon salt
1/4 teaspoon cayenne pepper or
    other ground red chile pepper
1 tablespoon water
1 plantain, sliced 1/2-inch thick
1/4 cup peanut oil

Mix the ginger, salt, cayenne pepper and water in a shallow dish. Add the plantain slices, turning to coat well.

Heat the oil in a nonstick skillet until almost smoking. Add the plantain slices a few at a time, cooking until golden brown on both sides and turning once; drain.

Serves four

If you know whence you came, there is really no limit to where you can go. —James Baldwin, American author

Injera
Flat Bread

8 cups self-rising flour   *Ethiopia*
2 cups whole wheat flour
1 teaspoon baking powder
2 cups soda water

Mix the self-rising flour, whole wheat flour and baking powder in a bowl. Add the soda water and stir to form a smooth batter.

Heat a large nonstick skillet until a drop of water bounces on the skillet's surface. Add just enough batter to cover the bottom of the skillet, tilting the skillet to coat evenly. Bake until the moisture has evaporated and small holes appear on the surface; do not turn or cook until crisp. Remove and stack on a platter, covering with a cloth to prevent drying out.

To serve, arrange in overlapping concentric circles on a platter, beginning in the center. If served with stew, spoon the stew into the center of each bread and fold for individual servings.

Serves six to eight

Twisted Cakes

Ghana

1/2 cup butter
1 cup sugar
1/2 teaspoon grated nutmeg
salt to taste
1 egg
2 cups flour
2 tablespoons (about) milk
1 cup vegetable oil or shortening

Cream the butter and sugar in a mixer bowl until light and fluffy. Combine the nutmeg, salt and egg in a bowl and mix well. Add to the creamed mixture and mix well.

Add the flour gradually, mixing well after each addition. Add the milk, 1 tablespoon at a time, mixing with a fork until the mixture forms a ball.

Roll 1/4 inch thick on a lightly floured surface. Cut into 1/2-inch wide strips. Braid the strips, using 3 strips at a time. Cut each braid into 1-inch pieces.

Fry the pastry pieces in the heated oil in a skillet until golden brown; drain. Serve hot or cooled.

Serves ten

There is no person who is not a member of a race, a group, a family of humankind. Nobody exists alone. We are each a part of a specific collective past.

—Eugenia Collier, American writer

Bananas Ghana

8 medium bananas   *Ghana*
1/4 cup sugar
1 teaspoon cinnamon
1 cup orange juice
3 tablespoons orange liqueur
1/4 cup shredded coconut
chopped peanuts (optional)
1 cup sour cream
2 tablespoons brown sugar

Cut the bananas into halves lengthwise, then crosswise. Combine the sugar and cinnamon in a shallow dish and mix well. Dip the banana pieces in the cinnamon-sugar, coating well. Arrange cut side down in a 9x9-inch baking pan.

Mix the orange juice and liqueur in a small bowl. Pour over the bananas. Bake at 350 degrees for 20 minutes, basting occasionally. Sprinkle the coconut and peanuts over the top. Combine the sour cream and brown sugar in a bowl and mix well. Spoon onto the bananas to serve.

Serves eight

38

Chlada Fakya
Dessert Fruit Salad

1/4 cantelope or honeydew, chopped   Algeria
2 apples, chopped
2 bananas, sliced
5 oranges, peeled, chopped, seeded
juice of 2 oranges
juice of 2 lemons
2 tablespoons sugar
1 tablespoon orange water (optional)
1 teaspoon vanilla extract
1/2 teaspoon cinnamon

Combine the melon, apples, bananas and oranges in a large bowl.
Sprinkle with the orange juice, lemon juice, sugar, orange water, vanilla and
cinnamon and mix gently. Chill until serving time.

Serves six

*The more you praise and celebrate your life, the more there
is in life to celebrate.*
—Oprah Winfrey, talk show host and actress

Cocada Amarela
Coconut Pudding

1 cup sugar
1 cup water
6 whole cloves
1 fresh coconut, grated
6 egg yolks
1/8 teaspoon cinnamon
2 egg whites, at room temperature (optional)
1/4 cup sugar

Angola

Combine 1 cup sugar, water and cloves in a large heavy saucepan and mix well. Cook over low heat until the sugar is completely dissolved, stirring constantly. Cook, covered, over medium heat for 2 to 3 minutes or until the steam washes the sugar crystals from the side of the pan. Cook, uncovered, over high heat to 230 degrees on a candy thermometer, or until a small spoonful dropped into cold water forms coarse threads. Remove the cloves with a slotted spoon and discard.

Reduce the heat to low. Stir in the coconut. Simmer for 10 to 12 minutes or until the coconut becomes translucent. Remove from the heat.

Beat the egg yolks and cinnamon in a mixer bowl until thick. Stir a small amount of the hot mixture into the beaten egg yolks; stir the egg yolks into the hot mixture. Cook over medium heat for 12 to 15 minutes or until thickened, stirring constantly. Spoon into 6 custard cups.

Beat the egg whites in a mixer bowl until soft peaks form. Add 1/4 cup sugar gradually, beating until stiff peaks form. Spread over the puddings, sealing to the edge of the cups. Bake at 350 degrees until the tops are light brown. Serve hot or chilled.

Serves six

Orange Dessert Salad

6 almonds, slivered   *Morocco*
2 tablespoons butter
6 oranges, sliced, seeded
6 large pitted dates, chopped
juice of 1/2 lemon
1 teaspoon cinnamon

Sauté the almonds in the butter in a skillet. Combine the almonds, oranges and dates in a large bowl. Stir in the lemon juice gently. Chill, covered, until serving time.

Spoon onto dessert plates. Sprinkle with the cinnamon.

Serves six

Groundnut Toffee
Peanut Toffee

1 1/4 cups sugar   *Ghana*
1 tablespoon butter
2 cups roasted peanuts

Sprinkle the sugar in a saucepan. Cook over low heat for 5 minutes or until melted and light brown. Add the butter and mix well. Stir in the peanuts. Cook for 5 minutes or until well coated.

Pour onto a dampened pastry board. Detach small spoonfuls with a wooden spoon and roll into balls. Let stand until cool. Store in an airtight container.

Makes two and one-half dozen

Ginger Beer

25 pieces ginger, peeled   *Liberia*
2 pineapples
2 teaspoons yeast (optional)
1 gallon boiling water
3$\frac{1}{2}$ cups molasses

    Pound the ginger. Cut the pineapple into chunks, leaving the peeling intact. Combine the ginger, pineapple and yeast in a large bowl. Pour the boiling water over the mixture. Let stand in refrigerator overnight.

    Strain the liquid into a large container. Stir in the molasses. Chill until serving time.

    Adjust the water or ginger or add sugar at serving time to suit individual tastes.

Serves twenty

Mint Tea

boiling water   *Morocco*
1 tablespoon China green tea
24 sugar cubes
1 handful fresh mint leaves, or 1 teaspoon rose water

    Rinse a 6-cup teapot with boiling water to warm it; discard the water. Place the tea leaves in the warmed teapot. Add 1/4 cup boiling water to rinse the tea leaves and discard the water.

    Add the sugar cubes and fill the teapot with boiling water. Add the fresh mint, stirring in immediately; leaves should not float on the surface. Let stand for 2 minutes. Serve in small glasses.

Serves six

...there is as much dignity in tilling a field as in writing a poem. —Booker T. Washington

The need for tillers in the fields brought Africans to the new colonies of the Americas. There the attributes symbolized by the Wisdom Knot enabled them to find the dignity to make a new life—a quilt of existence woven from the old and the new.

There, also, the culinary influences of traditional African cooking were incorporated into the cooking of the French, Spanish, Portuguese, and native cultures to create a cuisine with a broader palette. Sesame or benne, peanuts or groundnuts, cumin, okra, rice, and yams, long staples in the African diet, soon became valuable additions to diets in the American colonies.

Caribbean and South America
The Diaspora

NYANSAPƆ
(n-yahn-sah-pho)

Wisdom Knot

NYANSAPƆ is the symbol of
wisdom, ingenuity, intelligence, and patience.

Sardine Salad

    1 (3-ounce) can sardines, drained
    1¹/₂ teaspoons lime or lemon juice
    2 tablespoons olive oil
    1 garlic clove, crushed
    1¹/₂ teaspoons lime or lemon juice
    1 tablespoon grated onion
    ¹/₂ teaspoon salt
    ¹/₄ teaspoon chopped hot pepper
    1 cucumber, sliced (optional)

Arrange the sardines in a single layer in a dish. Drizzle with 1¹/₂ teaspoons lime juice.

Combine the olive oil, garlic and 1¹/₂ teaspoons lime juice in a bowl and mix well. Stir in the onion, salt and hot pepper. Spoon over the sardines. Let stand at room temperature for 20 to 30 minutes.

Arrange the cucumber slices around the edge of a serving platter. Spoon the sardines into the center.

Serves two or three

Salade de Chou Palmiste
Hearts of Palm Salad

    1 (14-ounce) can hearts of palm, drained   Martinique
    juice of 1 lime
    salt and freshly ground pepper to taste

Slice the hearts of palm lengthwise into narrow strips and place in a bowl. Drizzle with the lime juice. Season with salt and pepper.

Serves two or three

Pepper Pot Soup

8 ounces salt beef or pig's tail,   *Jamaica*
    cut into bite-size pieces (optional)
2 vegetable or chicken bouillon cubes
2 quarts water
2 cups coconut milk
8 ounces taro, peeled, cut into chunks
8 ounces yams, peeled, cut into chunks
8 ounces sweet potatoes, peeled, cut into chunks
2 scallions, finely chopped
2 Scotch bonnet chiles, seeded, finely chopped
1 pound smoked mackerel steaks, cut into chunks
1/4 bunch spinach or Swiss chard, julienned
leaves of 1/2 bunch celery, julienned
salt and freshly ground pepper to taste

Combine the salt beef, bouillon cubes and water in a stockpot. Bring to a boil. Boil for 20 minutes or until the beef is almost tender.

Add the coconut milk, taro, yams, sweet potatoes, scallions and chiles and mix well. Bring to a boil and reduce the heat. Simmer for 30 minutes, stirring occasionally.

Stir in the mackerel, spinach and celery leaves. Simmer for 20 to 30 minutes or until the vegetables are tender and the soup is of the desired consistency, stirring occasionally. Season with salt and pepper. Ladle into warmed soup bowls.

Serves four to six

Sopa de Feijão
Black Bean Soup

1 cup dried black beans   *Brazil*
4 ounces salt pork or slab bacon
8 ounces lean beef, coarsely chopped (optional)
3 quarts water
1 carrot, finely chopped
2 yellow onions, finely chopped
1 fresh melegueta or other fresh or pickled red or
    green chile
2 to 3 teaspoons salt
1 teaspoon sage, crushed
1/2 teaspoon mace or ground cloves
ground black pepper to taste

Sort and rinse the beans. Combine with enough water to cover by several inches in a bowl. Let stand for 8 to 10 hours; drain. Blanch the salt pork in simmering water in a saucepan for 2 minutes. Drain and chop the salt pork.

Fry the salt pork and beef in a heavy saucepan or stockpot over high heat for 8 minutes or until brown on all sides; drain.

Stir in the beans, 3 quarts water, carrot, onions, melegueta, salt, sage, mace and black pepper. Bring to a boil and reduce the heat. Simmer, covered, for 1 1/2 hours or until the beans are tender, stirring occasionally.

Press the soup through a coarse-mesh sieve or food mill. Return the soup to the stockpot. Cook just until heated through, stirring occasionally. Ladle into soup bowls.

Serves four

Pepper Salad

2 large green bell peppers, sliced into rounds
2 large yellow bell peppers, sliced into rounds
2 large red bell peppers, sliced into rounds
2 large yellow tomatoes, thinly sliced
2 large red tomatoes, thinly sliced
1 head iceberg lettuce, julienned
Lime Vinaigrette

Layer the green peppers, yellow peppers, red peppers, yellow tomatoes, red tomatoes and lettuce in the order listed in a large salad bowl. Drizzle with the Lime Vinaigrette; do not toss.

Cut into wedges and place on individual salad plates. Serve with hot crusty bread.

Lime Vinaigrette

1/4 cup extra-light olive oil
juice of 1 lime
1/2 bunch basil, julienned
1 tablespoon wine vinegar or apple cider vinegar
1/2 teaspoon paprika
1/2 teaspoon sugar
1/8 teaspoon dry mustard
salt and freshly ground pepper to taste

Combine the olive oil, lime juice, basil, wine vinegar, paprika, sugar, dry mustard, salt and pepper in a jar with a tightfitting lid. Shake to mix.

Serves four

Goat Curry

2 pounds lean boneless goat meat, chopped   *Jamaica*
2 Scotch bonnet or other hot chiles,
   finely chopped
3 to 4 tablespoons curry powder
2 garlic cloves, finely chopped
2 scallions, finely chopped
2 tablespoons vegetable oil
1 tablespoon (heaping) cornstarch
salt to taste
1/4 cup corn oil or olive oil
2 tablespoons ghee (clarified butter)
2 large onions, finely chopped
4 large tomatoes, blanched, peeled, chopped
1 quart water
freshly ground black pepper to taste

Combine the goat meat, chiles, curry powder, garlic, scallions, vegetable oil, cornstarch and salt in a bowl and mix well. Marinate, covered, in the refrigerator for 3 to 10 hours, stirring occasionally; the longer the marinating time the better the flavor. Drain, reserving the marinade.

Heat the corn oil and ghee in a nonstick skillet over medium heat. Add the goat and sauté until brown on all sides. Add the onions. Sauté for 3 to 4 minutes.

Stir in the reserved marinade, tomatoes, water and black pepper. Bring to a boil and reduce the heat. Season with salt and pepper. Simmer for 1 to 1 1/2 hours or until the goat is tender and the sauce has been reduced to a creamy thin consistency. Serve with hot cooked rice, fried plantains and chutney.

Serves four

Griots de Porc
Braised Pork

1 cup fresh lime juice

Haiti

1 pound pork loin, cut into 1-inch pieces
$1/2$ cup fresh orange juice
1 large onion, minced
5 chives, minced
1 Scotch bonnet chile, minced
2 garlic cloves, minced
salt and freshly ground black pepper to taste

Drizzle $1/2$ cup of the lime juice over the pork in a bowl and toss to coat. Mix the remaining $1/2$ cup lime juice, orange juice, onion, chives, chile, garlic, salt and black pepper in a bowl. Add to the pork, tossing to coat.

Marinate, covered, in the refrigerator for 1 hour or longer, stirring occasionally. Spoon the mixture into a cast-iron skillet. Add enough cold water to cover the pork.

Bring to a boil over medium heat and reduce the heat. Simmer until the pork is cooked through and the sauce is thickened, stirring occasionally. Serve with hot cooked rice.

Serves four

Jerk Pork

4 red chiles, chopped, or ¼ cup hot chile paste   *Jamaica*
2 onions, chopped
1 large piece of gingerroot, peeled, grated
½ cup vegetable oil
¼ cup soy sauce
1 teaspoon allspice
1 teaspoon garlic salt
3 bay leaves
3 pounds thickly sliced pork fillets
½ cup water

Process the chiles, onions and gingerroot in a blender or food processor until puréed. Add the oil, soy sauce, allspice, garlic salt and bay leaves and process until mixed.

Rub the pork on all sides with the chile mixture. Place in a dish and marinate, covered, in the refrigerator for 8 to 10 hours. Drain, reserving the marinade.

Grill the pork over hot coals or bake in a 350-degree oven until cooked through.

Mix the reserved marinade and water in a saucepan. Simmer over low heat for 10 to 15 minutes or until of a sauce consistency, stirring frequently. Serve with the pork. Add a green salad, sweet potatoes, rice or breadfruit for a meal or serve with drinks as an appetizer.

You may sprinkle small amounts of cinnamon sticks, chicory, basil or other herbs on the hot coals so the pork absorbs these flavors.

Serves four to six

Asopao de Pollo
Chicken and Rice

1 teaspoon oregano
1 garlic clove, minced
salt to taste
1 (2- to 3-pound) chicken, cut up
2 tablespoons lard
⅓ cup chopped cooked ham
2 medium tomatoes, chopped
1 medium onion, chopped
1 medium green bell pepper, chopped
1½ quarts water
¼ cup chopped pimento-stuffed olives
1 tablespoon capers
2 cups uncooked rice
1 cup cooked peas
4 pimentos, julienned
½ cup freshly grated Parmesan cheese

Puerto Rico

Mix the oregano, garlic and salt in a small bowl. Rub the chicken with the mixture.

Heat the lard in a heavy saucepan until hot. Add the chicken. Cook until brown on all sides. Stir in the ham, tomatoes, onion and green pepper. Simmer, covered, for 30 minutes or until the chicken is cooked through, stirring occasionally. Cool slightly.

Remove and chop the chicken, discarding the skin and bones. Return the chicken to the saucepan and mix well. Stir in the water, olives and capers. Cook for 5 minutes, stirring occasionally.

Add the rice and mix well. Simmer until the rice is tender but moist, stirring occasionally. Serve immediately or the dish will lose its characteristic soupy consistency. Top each serving with peas and pimentos. Sprinkle with the cheese.

Serves six to eight

Fried Chicken

2 1/2 pounds cut-up chicken   *Jamaica*
1/2 yellow onion, sliced
3 green onions with tops, chopped
1 (1-inch) piece of gingerroot, peeled, chopped
3 sprigs of thyme, chopped, or
    2 teaspoons dried thyme, crushed
1 Scotch bonnet or other fresh chile, or
    1 teaspoon red hot pepper sauce
1 cup chicken stock
1 cup flour
1 tablespoon paprika
1 tablespoon garlic powder
1 teaspoon salt
1/2 teaspoon cayenne pepper
1/2 teaspoon ground white pepper
peanut oil for deep-frying

Cut the chicken parts into halves, discarding the skin. Combine the chicken, yellow onion, green onions, gingerroot, thyme, chile and chicken stock in bowl and mix well. Marinate, covered, in the refrigerator for 8 to 10 hours, turning occasionally. Drain, discarding the marinade.

Mix the flour, paprika, garlic powder, salt, cayenne and white pepper in a shallow dish or sealable plastic bag. Coat the chicken with the flour mixture.

Add enough peanut oil to a deep-fryer or heavy saucepan to measure 3 inches. Heat to 375 degrees. Add the chicken in batches and fry for 15 minutes or until brown and crisp and cooked through; drain. Serve immediately.

Serves four

Chicharrón de Pollo
Fried Marinated Chicken

1 (2- to 3-pound) chicken
1/4 cup fresh lime juice
1 tablespoon ginger soy sauce
salt to taste
1 cup flour
1/2 teaspoon paprika
freshly ground pepper to taste
1 1/2 cups vegetable oil
lemon slices

Dominican Republic

Cut the chicken into 16 pieces by dividing the wings, thighs, breasts and legs into halves. Arrange in a single layer in a dish.

Mix the lime juice, soy sauce and salt in a bowl. Pour over the chicken, turning to coat. Marinate, covered, in the refrigerator for 5 hours or longer.

Combine the flour, paprika, salt and pepper in a sealable plastic bag. Add the chicken in batches, shaking to coat.

Heat the oil to 325 degrees in a cast-iron skillet. Add the chicken in batches. Fry for 6 minutes per side or until golden brown; drain. Serve with lemon slices.

Serves four to six

Curried Chicken Rasta-Style

1 large onion, chopped
3 tablespoons curry powder
1 tablespoon salt
1 tablespoon paprika
1 tablespoon turmeric
1½ teaspoons seasoned salt
1 teaspoon thyme
2 garlic cloves, minced, or 2 teaspoons garlic powder
1 (2-pound) chicken, cut up
virgin olive oil
⅛ teaspoon curry powder
1 medium onion, chopped
½ cup boiling water
2 large potatoes, peeled, cut into quarters
1 red apple, peeled, chopped
1 large tomato, chopped
½ cup sliced mushrooms

Combine 1 large onion, 3 tablespoons curry powder, salt, paprika, turmeric, seasoned salt, thyme and garlic in a bowl and mix well. Add the chicken, tossing to coat. Marinate, covered, in the refrigerator for 8 to 10 hours, turning occasionally.

Brown the chicken on all sides in olive oil and ⅛ teaspoon curry powder in a skillet. Transfer to a large saucepan and add 1 medium onion and the boiling water. Cook for 20 minutes, stirring occasionally.

Add the potatoes, apple, tomato and mushrooms. Cook until the vegetables are tender and the chicken is cooked through, stirring occasionally. Serve over hot cooked rice or a mixture of rice and peas with Mango Chutney (page 73).

Serves eight

Caribbean Chicken Stew

1 chicken, cut up
1 teaspoon vinegar
1 tablespoon salt
1 teaspoon black pepper
2 garlic cloves, crushed
2 teaspoons vinegar
1 tablespoon ginger powder
1/4 cup vegetable oil
1 large onion, sliced
4 tomatoes, chopped
1/4 cup tomato paste
1 hot pepper, chopped (optional)
4 cups boiling water
1/2 cup deveined peeled shrimp
1/2 cup peanut butter
1 cup unsalted peanuts

Rinse the chicken in a mixture of 1 teaspoon vinegar and cold water in a bowl; drain. Arrange in a single layer in a dish. Sprinkle with 1 tablespoon salt, black pepper and half the garlic. Drizzle with 2 teaspoons vinegar. Marinate, covered, in the refrigerator for 1 to 2 hours. Drain and pat dry. Sprinkle with the ginger. Fry the chicken in the oil in a skillet until brown on all sides. Remove to a platter with a slotted spoon, reserving the pan drippings.

Sauté the onion and remaining garlic in the reserved pan drippings until light brown. Stir in the tomatoes, tomato paste and hot pepper. Cook for 3 minutes, stirring frequently. Add the boiling water, shrimp and peanut butter. Return the chicken to the skillet.

Cook for 45 minutes or until the chicken is cooked through, stirring occasionally. Adjust the seasonings.

Spread the peanuts on a baking sheet. Broil until toasted. Stir into the stew 15 minutes before the end of the cooking process. Garnish with chopped parsley and hot cooked rice.

Serves four or five

Codfish and Ackee

1 pound salted codfish

2 onions, chopped

3 tablespoons vegetable oil

4 ounces bacon, chopped, or smoked ham hock

2 red or green bell peppers, chopped

3 tomatoes, chopped

finely chopped fresh basil, or a pinch of dried oregano

salt and black pepper to taste

1 (15- to 19-ounce) can ackee, drained

Jamaica

Soak the fish in cold water to cover in a bowl for 10 to 12 hours, changing the water several times. Drain and rinse the fish.

Combine with fresh water to cover in a saucepan and bring to a boil. Reduce the heat to medium and cook for 20 to 30 minutes or until the fish flakes easily. Drain and cool. Flake the fish and set aside, discarding any bones.

Sauté the onions in the oil in a skillet for 3 minutes. Add the bacon, bell peppers, tomatoes, basil, salt and black pepper. Cook for 3 to 5 minutes, stirring frequently.

Add the flaked fish. Cook for 5 to 10 minutes. Stir in the ackee. Cook for 10 minutes longer, stirring gently. Serve hot with rice and additional tomatoes, onion, parsley and/or cilantro.

Ackee is a bright red tropical fruit with three large black seeds and a soft creamy white flesh.

Serves four

Salted Cod Cakes

1 pound (about) salt cod
1 potato, cooked, mashed
1 small onion, grated
2 garlic cloves, crushed
1 teaspoon lemon juice
1/4 fresh hot pepper, chopped
1/4 teaspoon chopped fresh thyme
1/4 teaspoon salt, or to taste
1 egg
1 tablespoon (about) milk
1/4 cup flour
1/4 cup bread crumbs
vegetable oil for frying

Soak the fish in a bowl of cold water for 4 to 5 hours; drain. Remove the skin and bones. Pat the cod dry with a tea towel. Shred enough of the fish to measure 2 cups.

Combine with the potato in a bowl and mix well. Stir in the onion, garlic, lemon juice, hot pepper, thyme and salt. Whisk the egg lightly in a bowl. Whisk in the milk. Add the egg mixture to the cod mixture and mix well.

Shape into small balls with lightly floured hands, adding additional milk if needed for the desired consistency. Mix 1/4 cup flour and bread crumbs in a shallow dish. Roll the balls in the flour mixture.

Fry in hot oil in a skillet until golden brown; drain. Serve as a main dish or with avocado dip as an appetizer.

Serves six to eight

Fondue Marinière
Seafood Fondue

2 cups coconut oil   *Guadeloupe*
2 cups peanut oil
1 pound red snapper, cut into 1-inch pieces
1 pound kingfish or whiting fillets, cut into 1-inch pieces
1 pound tuna, cut into 1-inch pieces
2 sweet potatoes, peeled, cut into 1-inch pieces

Combine the coconut oil and peanut oil in a fondue pot. Bring to a boil over medium heat. Place over the fondue burner.

Arrange equal portions of the fish and sweet potatoes on 6 to 8 plates along with the desired dipping sauces. Proceed as for any fondue.

Serves six to eight

Curried Lobster Salad

1 head Bibb lettuce, separated
1 medium tomato, sliced
1 pound cooked lobster tail meat
6 tablespoons mayonnaise
1/2 very ripe avocado, chopped
1 tablespoon coconut cream
1 teaspoon fresh lime juice
1/8 teaspoon hot pepper sauce

Arrange the lettuce and tomato slices on 4 plates. Top with the lobster meat.

Process the mayonnaise, avocado, coconut cream, lime juice and hot pepper sauce in a blender until smooth. Drizzle over the salad. Serve immediately.

Serves four

Arroz Negro con Calamares
Black Rice with Calamari

7 ounces uncooked wild black rice   *Cuba*
1/4 cup olive oil
1 onion, julienned
2 garlic cloves, finely chopped
1/2 to 1 cup fresh thyme
1 cup clear fish stock
1 cup red wine
1 cup coconut milk
salt and pepper to taste
1 cup clear fish stock (optional)
1 cup coconut milk (optional)
1 pound fresh calamari, sliced
4 lemon slices
2 tablespoons chopped fresh chives

Combine the wild rice with enough cold water to cover in a bowl. Let stand for several minutes. Drain and rinse; drain again.

Heat the olive oil in a nonstick saucepan or skillet. Add the onion, garlic and thyme and sauté for 4 to 5 minutes or until the onion is light brown.

Stir in 1 cup stock, red wine and 1 cup coconut milk. Bring to a boil. Stir in the rice. Season with salt and pepper. Simmer, covered, for 1 hour, stirring occasionally. Add 1 cup stock and 1 cup coconut milk if most of the liquid has been absorbed during the first hour of cooking. Cook for 15 minutes.

Add the calamari and cook for 10 to 15 minutes or until tender. Serve hot with a slice of lemon on the side of each serving and a sprinkling of chives on top.

Serves four

Jerk Seasoning

Jamaica

1/2 cup allspice berries
1 (1-inch) cinnamon stick, broken
2 teaspoons nutmeg
10 scallions with tops, minced
1 medium onion, minced
3 Scotch bonnet chiles, seeded, minced
2 tablespoons dark Jamaican rum
salt and freshly ground black pepper to taste

Spread the allspice berries on a baking sheet. Bake at 350 degrees for 5 minutes. Grind the berries, cinnamon and nutmeg in a spice mill.

Combine the spice powder, scallions, onion, chiles, rum, salt and pepper in a mortar. Pound with a pestle until a thick paste forms. Use as a marinade for pork or chicken.

Makes two cups

Caribbean Spice Blend

1 tablespoon paprika
1 teaspoon ground ginger
1 teaspoon cumin, or 3/4 teaspoon whole cumin seeds
1 teaspoon cayenne pepper or ground red chile pepper
1/2 teaspoon each salt and crushed thyme
1/4 teaspoon each ground white or black pepper, allspice
    and turmeric

Mix all the ingredients in a bowl. Store at room temperature in an airtight container.

Use as a rub for 2 to 3 pounds of beef, pork, fish or poultry. Let stand for 30 minutes before baking or grilling. You may add any of the following spices: cinnamon, ground cloves, garlic powder, red pepper flakes, cardamom, freshly grated nutmeg, ground annatto seeds, coriander and/or mace.

Makes one-fourth cup

Feijão com Camarões
Bean Stew with Prawns

1 pound dried black-eyed beans   *Brazil*
salt to taste
3 large onions, julienned
1 cup palm oil
10 ounces fresh tomatoes, blanched, peeled, chopped
2 or 3 fresh red chiles, chopped (optional)
7 ounces dried prawns

Combine the black-eyed beans with enough cold water to cover by several inches in a bowl. Let stand for 8 to 10 hours. Drain and rinse.

Combine the beans with enough water to cover by several inches in a saucepan and add the salt. Cook for 30 to 40 minutes or until the beans are tender but not mushy, stirring occasionally; drain.

Sauté the onions in the palm oil in a saucepan until golden brown. Stir in the tomatoes and chiles. Cook over medium heat for 3 minutes, stirring constantly.

Add the dried prawns and mix well. Simmer for 3 minutes, stirring frequently. Mix in the beans. Simmer for 10 to 15 minutes longer, stirring occasionally.

Serve with grilled or fried plantains or bananas, boiled brown or white rice, coarsely grated dry-baked cassava or farinha de mandioca (coarse cassava powder).

Serves four

Calalou with Shrimp

Guadeloupe

1 pound calalou (taro) leaves,
    Chinese spinach or plain spinach
1 bouquet sorrel leaves
3 cups water
½ teaspoon salt (optional)
1 pound shrimp, peeled, deveined
1 bouquet garni
2 medium yellow onions, chopped
2 garlic cloves, minced
8 ounces bacon, chopped
1 pimento, seeded, chopped
1 tablespoon vegetable oil

Remove the stems and large veins from the calalou and sorrel leaves. Rinse with cold water.

Combine the water and salt in a stockpot. Add the calalou leaves, sorrel leaves, shrimp and bouquet garni. Bring to a boil and reduce the heat. Simmer for 25 minutes or until very tender, stirring occasionally.

Sauté the onions, garlic, bacon and pimento in the oil in a large skillet until the onions are tender. Stir into the calalou. Simmer for 20 minutes longer, stirring occasionally; do not boil. Discard the bouquet garni. Serve immediately.

Tie 2 tablespoons chopped fresh parsley, 2 tablespoons chopped fresh chives and 1 tablespoon chopped fresh thyme in cheesecloth for a bouquet garni.

Serves four

Curried Coconut Shrimp

2 pounds large shrimp, peeled, deveined
1 red bell pepper, finely chopped
2 garlic cloves, finely chopped
1 Scotch bonnet chile, seeded, finely chopped
1/4 cup olive oil
1 tablespoon mild curry powder
2 cups coconut milk
salt to taste
1 small bunch cilantro, leaves only, finely chopped

Cook the shrimp, red pepper, garlic and chile in the olive oil in a saucepan or skillet over medium heat for 3 to 4 minutes, stirring constantly.

Stir in the curry powder. Cook for 1 minute, stirring constantly. Add the coconut milk and mix well. Season with salt. Increase the heat to high. Cook for 10 minutes or until thickened, stirring constantly.

Stir in the cilantro. Serve immediately with Sweet Potato Fries. Top generously with additional cilantro leaves.

Serves four

Sweet Potato Fries

2 sweet potatoes, peeled, cut into long flat strips
salt and freshly ground pepper
vegetable oil for deep-frying

Sprinkle the sweet potatoes with salt and pepper. Heat oil in a large saucepan over medium heat until hot but not smoking. Fry the sweet potatoes in batches in the hot oil for 1 to 2 minutes or until cooked through and crisp; drain.

Serves four

Aubergine à la Tomate
Eggplant with Tomatoes

2 ounces bacon, chopped
1 tablespoon vegetable oil or butter
1 onion, finely chopped
2 garlic cloves, chopped
1 (1-pound) eggplant, peeled, cut into 1-inch cubes
1 pound tomatoes, peeled, chopped
1 teaspoon chopped fresh hot red or green chile pepper
salt to taste

Martinique

Sauté the bacon in the oil in a saucepan. Add the onion and garlic and mix well. Sauté until the onion is tender but not brown.

Stir in the eggplant and tomatoes. Cook, covered, for 15 minutes, stirring occasionally; remove the cover. Cook for 15 minutes longer or until most of the liquid has evaporated, stirring frequently. Stir in the hot pepper and salt.

Serves six

If we love ourselves, we love Africa and the Caribbean. We are indissolubly joined. —Randall Robinson

Coo-Coo
Steamed Cornmeal and Okra

6 cups chicken stock or beef stock   *Tobago*
salt to taste
12 small okra pods, cut into 1/4-inch slices
2 cups yellow cornmeal
2 tablespoons unsalted butter, softened
1 pound sweet potatoes, peeled, cooked, sliced
2 medium tomatoes, peeled, sliced
2 pimentos, sliced
lettuce leaves

Bring the chicken stock to a boil in a large saucepan. Stir in the salt. Add the okra. Cook, covered, for 10 minutes.

Add the cornmeal gradually to the stock mixture in a steady stream, stirring constantly with a wooden spoon. Cook over medium heat for 5 minutes or until thick and smooth, stirring constantly.

Place the butter in a heated bowl, tilting the bowl to coat the bottom and side. Add the cornmeal mixture, shaking and turning the bowl until the mixture forms a ball and absorbs the butter. Place on a heated serving platter. Arrange the sweet potatoes, tomatoes, pimentos and lettuce around the Coo-Coo.

Serves six

Arroz Baiana
Bahian Rice

2 cups uncooked long grain white rice   *Brazil*
1/2 yellow onion, finely chopped (optional)
1 garlic clove, minced (optional)
2 tablespoons vegetable oil
1/2 teaspoon salt
3 3/4 cups hot water

Combine the rice with enough water to cover by 1 inch in a bowl and stir. Let stand for 1 minute; drain.

Sauté the onion and garlic in the oil in a saucepan over medium heat for 3 minutes or until tender. Stir in the rice. Cook for 4 to 5 minutes or until the rice is opaque but not brown. Add the salt and hot water and mix well.

Cook over medium heat for 12 minutes or until the water is absorbed. Remove from the heat and let stand, covered, for 10 minutes before serving.

For Arroz con Coco, substitute a mixture of 3 cups coconut milk and 3/4 cup water for the 3 3/4 cups water.

Serves six to eight

We do not choose our cultures, we belong to them.
—Aime Cesaire, Martinican writer

Roti
Crepes

2 cups unbleached flour   *Guyana*
1/4 teaspoon baking powder
1/4 teaspoon salt
corn oil
unbleached flour

Sift 2 cups flour, baking powder and salt into a bowl and mix well. Add just enough water to make a stiff dough and mix well. Shape the dough into 4 to 6 balls.

Roll each ball until flat on a lightly floured surface. Spread each with corn oil and sprinkle lightly with flour. Fold back into balls by turning the edges in on each other. Let stand for 30 minutes or longer.

Roll each ball into a very thin circle on a lightly floured surface. Bake on a griddle or in a heavy cast-iron skillet for 3 minutes or until light brown, drizzling the top side with a small amount of corn oil and turning frequently.

Remove each roti from the griddle as it browns and clap in the palms of the hands 2 or 3 times. Serve hot with chicken curry and homemade chutney.

Serves four to six

Sweet Bread

8 ounces finely shredded coconut   *Tobago*
1/2 cup coconut milk
3 cups flour
1/2 cup packed brown sugar
2 teaspoons allspice
2 teaspoons baking powder
2 teaspoons dry yeast
1 teaspoon nutmeg
1/8 teaspoon salt
1 1/2 cups (120-degree) coconut milk
1/2 cup butter, softened
1/2 cup raisins

Combine the coconut and 1/2 cup coconut milk in a bowl and mix well. Let stand for 30 minutes.

Mix the flour, brown sugar, allspice, baking powder, yeast, nutmeg and salt in a bowl and mix well. Stir in 1 1/2 cups heated coconut milk. Add the undrained coconut, butter and raisins and mix well. Spoon the batter into a greased and floured loaf pan.

Bake at 350 degrees for 1 to 1 1/2 hours or until the edges pull from the sides of the pan, the top is golden brown and a wooden pick inserted in the center comes out clean. Remove to a wire rack to cool.

Makes one loaf

Bolinhos de Estudante
Coconut Fritters

Brazil

1 cup water
1/2 cup milk
1/2 cup quick-cooking tapioca
1/2 cup sugar
1/2 cup unsweetened finely grated dried coconut
salt to taste
1/2 teaspoon vanilla extract
peanut oil for deep-frying
cinnamon and sugar to taste

Combine the water, milk, tapioca, 1/2 cup sugar, coconut and salt in a saucepan. Cook over medium heat just until bubbles begin to form around the edge, stirring constantly; reduce the heat to low.

Cook for 5 minutes or until thickened, stirring constantly. Add the vanilla and mix well.

Remove from the heat and let stand until cool. Shape the cooled mixture into six 3-inch-long football shapes.

Heat 3 1/2 inches of peanut oil to 375 degrees in a deep fryer, heavy saucepan or wok. Add the fritters 1 or 2 at a time. Fry for 3 minutes or until brown on all sides; drain and cool slightly. Sprinkle with cinnamon and additional sugar. Serve immediately.

Serves six

Brown Sugar Fudge

2 cups packed light brown sugar.   *Barbados*
2/3 cup milk
2 tablespoons light corn syrup
1/4 teaspoon salt
2 tablespoons unsalted butter
1 tablespoon rum
1 teaspoon vanilla extract

Combine the brown sugar, milk, corn syrup and salt in a saucepan and mix well. Cook over medium heat until the brown sugar dissolves completely, stirring constantly. Continue cooking until the mixture registers 234 degrees on a candy thermometer, soft-ball stage, stirring occasionally. Remove from the heat.

Stir in the butter. Cool to 120 degrees; do not stir. Add the rum and vanilla. Beat with a wooden spoon until the mixture thickens and loses its luster.

Spread in a buttered 9x9-inch dish. Let stand until cool. Cut into 1-inch squares. Store, covered, in the refrigerator for up to 2 weeks.

Makes three dozen (one-inch) squares

Coconut Crème Brûlée

1 cup coconut milk
1 vanilla bean
1 cup light cream
3 eggs
¼ cup superfine sugar
6 tablespoons brown sugar
3 tablespoons water

Combine the coconut milk and vanilla bean in a saucepan. Cook over low heat for 5 minutes or until hot; do not boil. Let stand for 10 minutes to cool and allow the vanilla flavor to blend with the coconut milk. Remove and discard the vanilla bean.

Process the cream, eggs and sugar in a blender until smooth. Add the coconut milk. Process for 3 to 5 seconds. Pour into 4 ramekins.

Place the ramekins in a larger baking dish. Add enough water to reach halfway up the sides of the ramekins. Bake at 325 degrees for 30 to 40 minutes or until set.

Remove the ramekins from the water bath. Cool to room temperature on a wire rack. Chill, covered, for 8 to 10 hours.

Combine the brown sugar and water in a saucepan. Bring to a boil over medium heat. Cook for 5 to 7 minutes or until the brown sugar dissolves and the mixture turns pale golden brown, stirring constantly. Pour immediately over the top of each chilled custard; the caramel syrup will harden instantly. Chill for 2 to 3 hours longer.

Serve cold topped with sliced fresh fruit or small edible flowers. You may also bake this in an 8x8-inch baking dish; increase the baking time to 1 hour.

Serves four

Gâteau avec Citron et Mango
Lemon and Mango Dessert

8 ounces graham crackers or
   plain sweet cookies
$1/2$ cup melted butter
1 teaspoon cinnamon
$1/2$ teaspoon allspice
8 ounces fresh or drained canned mango pulp
$1/2$ cup fresh lemon juice
$1/2$ cup superfine sugar
2 egg yolks, lightly beaten
1 ounce unflavored gelatin
grated zest of 2 lemons
1 cup whipping cream
2 egg whites
4 pieces candied angelica
2 lemons, thinly sliced

Guadeloupe

Process the graham crackers in a food processor until finely crushed. Combine with the butter, cinnamon and allspice in a bowl and mix well. Press over the bottom and up the side of a greased 8-inch springform pan. Chill in the refrigerator.

Process the mango pulp in a food processor or blender until smooth. Combine with the lemon juice, sugar, egg yolks, gelatin and lemon zest in a double boiler and mix well. Cook over boiling water over medium heat until thickened, stirring constantly. Let stand until cool.

Beat the whipping cream in a mixer bowl until soft peaks form. Beat the egg whites in a mixer bowl until soft peaks form. Fold the egg whites and then the whipped cream into the mango mixture.

Spoon the mango filling into the prepared pan. Chill, covered, until set. Top with the angelica and lemon slices.

Serves four

Mango Chutney

2 cups mango pulp   *Guyana*
1 garlic clove
1 Scotch bonnet chile
1 (1-inch) piece gingerroot, peeled
1/4 teaspoon salt
1/2 cup cane vinegar
1/2 cup Demerara sugar or packed light brown sugar

Process the mango pulp, garlic, chile, gingerroot and salt in a food processor or blender until puréed. Transfer to a nonreactive saucepan.

Stir in the vinegar and sugar. Bring to a boil, stirring occasionally and reduce the heat. Simmer for 25 minutes or until thickened, stirring occasionally. Let stand until cool.

Store in the refrigerator for up to a month or spoon into sterilized jars and seal with 2-pieces lids to store for up to 6 months.

Makes one and one-half cups

The people with whom we have contact are the chisels and hammers that craft what we will become. Our life's journey is an ever-unfolding work of art that tells the story of where we have been and with whom we have traveled.
        —Iyanla Vanzant, American-born Yoruban priestess and writer

Coffee Tia Maria

1¼ cups freshly brewed Jamaican Blue   *Jamaica*
    Mountain coffee or other arabica coffee
⅓ cup packed brown sugar
¼ cup Tia Maria
⅓ cup dark rum
4 tablespoons light cream
chocolate shavings

Combine the coffee, brown sugar, Tia Maria and rum in a saucepan. Cook over low heat until the brown sugar dissolves and the mixture is hot, stirring to mix well; do not boil.

Pour into 2 heatproof glasses, filling ¾ full. Place a spoon lightly on the surface of the coffee and carefully pour 2 tablespoons cream down the curve of the spoon to float on the surface of each serving. Garnish with chocolate shavings.

Serves two

Nothing in the universe is attained by doing nothing. You must always give up something to get something. It's extremely basic, you can't fill a cup without giving up its contents first. You can't even move to a new place in the room without giving up the space you occupy. In other words sacrifice is a basic concept of our universe.
                         —Traditional Afro-Cuban rite

Dominica Rum Punch

Dominican Republic

1 green lime rind
3 cups dark rum
1 cup fresh lime juice
2 cups packed brown sugar
4 cups cold water
1 tablespoon angostura bitters
1 nutmeg, grated
lime slices

Soak the lime rind in the rum in a jar or shaker for 30 minutes. Add the lime juice and shake to mix.

Dissolve the brown sugar in the water in a jar. Add to the rum mixture. Add the bitters and shake to mix well. Sprinkle with the nutmeg.

Strain over ice in glasses. Garnish with lime slices.

Serves eight

Mango Daiquiri

Cuba

½ cup light rum
3 tablespoons superfine sugar
¼ cup orange liqueur
2 tablespoons fresh lime juice
¼ cup fresh mango juice
mint sprigs

Combine the rum, sugar, orange liqueur, lime juice and mango juice in a shaker and shake for 30 seconds.

Pour over crushed ice in 2 stemmed glasses. Garnish with mint sprigs.

Serves two

Spirit is an invisible force made visible in all life.
—Maya Angelou

  The spirit of survival visible in all life enabled early Africans in America to adapt and so to overcome the adverse circumstances of their existence and to grow and become strong.
  The ingredients and cooking techniques of the homeland sustained the spirits as well as the bodies of Africans in the plantation economy of the South and were soon assimilated into the general cuisine of the area, where they remain to this day as the comfort food of people regardless of color.

Africans in America
Survival of the Spirit

NKYINKYIN
(n-chin-chin)

Twisting

NKYINKYIN is the symbol of toughness, adaptability, selfless devotion to service, and an ability to withstand hardships and difficulties.

Oxtail Soup

4 to 6 oxtails
4 quarts water or beef stock
1 medium onion, chopped
2 ribs celery, coarsely chopped
2 carrots, coarsely chopped
2 medium potatoes, peeled, coarsely chopped
2 turnips, coarsely chopped
1 bay leaf
salt and pepper to taste
garlic salt to taste

Rinse the oxtails, discarding any small bones. Combine the oxtails and water in a stockpot and cook until tender. Add the onion, celery, carrots, potatoes, turnips, bay leaf, salt, pepper and garlic salt and mix well.

Cook until the vegetables are tender and the soup is of the desired consistency, stirring occasionally. Discard the bay leaf.

Serves six to eight

The potential for strength, endurance, courage, inventiveness, and creativity exists in every human being God created.
—Michelle Wallace, American writer and critic

Chitterlings and Hog Maws

10 pounds frozen or fresh chitterlings
3 hog maws
1 cup vinegar
1 large onion
1 small potato, peeled
1 red pepper pod, crushed
1 garlic clove
2 tablespoons salt
1 teaspoon black pepper
1 bay leaf

Thaw the frozen chitterlings in the refrigerator for 4 to 5 hours.

Remove the outer lining of the chitterlings. Place under running water and pull away the waste parts and most of the fat.

Place the chitterlings and maws in a large stockpot with enough water to cover. Add the vinegar, onion, potato, red pepper, garlic, salt, black pepper and bay leaf and mix well. Bring to a boil over medium heat and reduce the heat.

Simmer for 4 to 5 hours, stirring occasionally. Drain, reserving some of the liquid and discarding the onion, potato and bay leaf.

Cut the hot chitterlings and maws into 2-inch pieces or desired serving sizes. Serve with the reserved liquid, hot sauce, additional salt and black pepper and/or additional vinegar.

Serves five to seven

Country-Style Pigs' Tails

12 fresh pigs' tails
1 tablespoon sugar
1 tablespoon margarine
2 cups water
2 garlic cloves, crushed
1 teaspoon salt
1/2 teaspoon pepper
1 onion, chopped
1 carrot, sliced
1 cup peas
1/2 cup chopped celery
1 tablespoon flour

Rinse the tails with cold water and pat dry. Heat the sugar in a skillet until brown, stirring constantly. Add the margarine. Cook until very hot, stirring constantly. Add the tails.

Cook until the tails are brown, stirring frequently. Stir in the water, garlic, salt and pepper. Bring to a boil.

Cook until tender, stirring occasionally. Add the onion, carrot, peas and celery and mix well. Cook until the vegetables are tender-crisp, stirring frequently.

Stir in a mixture of the flour and a small amount of warm water. Cook just until thickened, stirring constantly. Serve immediately.

This may also be prepared substituting 6 pigs' feet for the tails.

Serves four to six

Pigs' Feet

6 young tender pigs' feet
salt and black pepper to taste
cayenne pepper to taste
2 cups cider vinegar
3 blades mace
1 red pepper pod
2 bay leaves
12 whole cloves

Clean and scrape the pigs' feet. Soak in cold water in a bowl for several hours; drain. Split and crack the feet in several places.

Combine with enough cold water to cover in a stockpot. Simmer until tender; drain. Sprinkle with salt, black pepper and cayenne pepper and transfer to a crock.

Bring the vinegar, mace, red pepper, bay leaves and cloves to a boil in a saucepan. Boil for several minutes. Pour over the pigs' feet in the crock. Let stand, covered, in the refrigerator for 24 hours. Discard the bay leaves and cloves.

Serves six

Red Beans and Rice

1 (1-pound) package dried red beans or kidney beans
2 green bell peppers, chopped
1 large yellow onion, chopped
3 ribs celery, chopped
1 bunch green onions with tops, chopped
3 garlic cloves, chopped
2 tablespoons vegetable oil
salt and black pepper to taste
4 to 6 Creole or other spicy sausages,
    cut into 1/2-inch slices (optional)
1 garlic clove, minced
hot cooked rice
1 cup chopped fresh parsley

Sort and rinse the beans. Combine with enough water to cover by several inches in a bowl. Let stand for 8 to 10 hours; drain.

Combine the beans with enough water to cover by 6 inches in a stockpot. Bring to a boil and reduce the heat. Cook, partially covered, over medium-low heat for 1 1/2 to 2 hours or until the beans are tender.

Sauté the bell peppers, onion, celery, green onions and 3 garlic cloves in the oil in a skillet over medium-low heat for 30 minutes or until tender. Add the vegetable mixture to the beans and mix well. Season with salt and black pepper.

Brown the sausage in a skillet over medium heat. Add to the bean mixture and mix gently or serve on the side with the beans.

Simmer the beans for 15 minutes longer to allow the flavors to blend, stirring occasionally. Stir in 1 minced garlic clove 5 minutes before serving. Spoon over rice and sprinkle with the parsley.

Serves six

Chicken and Dumplings

1 hen or frying chicken, cut into 8 pieces
4 cups water
2 ribs celery, chopped or sliced
2 carrots, peeled, chopped
1 green bell pepper, chopped
1 yellow onion, chopped
2 garlic cloves, minced
1 bay leaf
1 tablespoon salt
1 tablespoon freshly ground black pepper
2½ cups flour
3 tablespoons sugar
2 teaspoons baking powder
1½ cups milk
3 eggs, beaten
½ cup shortening

Combine the chicken, water, celery, carrots, green pepper, onion, garlic, bay leaf, salt and black pepper in a stockpot. Bring to a boil over medium heat and reduce the heat. Simmer for 1½ to 2 hours for a hen and 45 to 60 minutes for a fryer or until tender.

Combine the flour, sugar and baking powder in a bowl and mix well. Make a well in the center of the dry ingredients. Add the milk, eggs and shortening to the well. Mix with a fork until a smooth soft dough forms. Turn onto a lightly floured surface. Shape into 1-inch balls with lightly floured hands.

Add hot water to the stockpot if necessary to cover the chicken and vegetables. Drop the dumplings into the hot liquid to cover the surface in a single layer. Cook, covered, for 10 to 20 minutes or until the dumplings are tender. Discard the bay leaf. Serve immediately.

Serves four or five

Chicken and Rice

> 1 large frying chicken or hen, cut up
> 2 or 3 slices bacon or ¼ cup butter
> salt and pepper to taste
> 2 cups uncooked rice
> 1 (10-ounce) can tomatoes (optional)
> 1 small onion, chopped (optional)
> 1 teaspoon sugar (if tomatoes are added)

Combine the chicken and bacon in a saucepan. Add enough boiling water to cover. Season generously with salt and pepper. Simmer, covered, until the chicken is tender; skim.

Stir in the rice, tomatoes, onion and sugar. Cook for 30 to 40 minutes longer or until the rice is tender, the liquid is absorbed and the mixture is thick enough to eat with a fork, stirring occasionally.

You may substitute sausage or finely chopped parboiled liver and kidneys for the chicken.

Serves four

Gumbo Filé

1 large chicken, cut up
salt and black pepper to taste
cayenne pepper to taste
2 tablespoons butter or 1 tablespoon lard
8 ounces lean ham, chopped
1 large onion, chopped
3 sprigs of parsley, chopped
1 sprig of thyme, chopped
2 quarts boiling water
2 quarts oyster liquid, heated
1 bay leaf, crushed
1/2 red pepper pod, seeded, cut into halves
3 dozen oysters
2 tablespoons filé
hot cooked rice

Sprinkle the chicken on all sides with salt, black pepper and cayenne pepper. Melt the butter in a stockpot. Add the chicken and ham and cook, covered, for 5 to 10 minutes, turning occasionally.

Stir in the onion, parsley and thyme. Cook until the onion is brown, stirring occasionally. Add the boiling water, oyster liquid, bay leaf and red pepper and mix well. Simmer for 1 hour, stirring occasionally.

Bring to a boil and add the oysters. Boil for 3 minutes or until the edges of the oysters curl. Remove from the heat. Add the filé gradually to the stockpot, stirring constantly to mix. Pour immediately into a heated tureen; do not reheat the gumbo once the filé is added for the best flavor. Serve approximately 2 spoonfuls of rice with each serving of the gumbo.

Serves six

Crispy Fried Catfish

6 small whole catfish or fillets, cleaned, skinned
1 cup yellow cornmeal
2 teaspoons paprika
1 teaspoon salt
1/4 teaspoon black pepper
1/8 teaspoon cayenne pepper (optional)
vegetable oil for frying

Rinse the fish with cold water and pat dry. Mix the cornmeal, paprika, salt, black pepper and cayenne pepper in a bowl. Coat the fish on all sides with the cornmeal mixture. Arrange in a single layer on a tray. Freeze for 5 minutes or chill for up to 2 hours.

Pour oil to measure 2 to 3 inches in a deep fryer or 1 1/2 to 2 inches in a heavy skillet. Heat the oil to 325 degrees or until hot. Add the fish and fry for 5 to 8 minutes on each side or until brown; drain.

Serves six

My great grandmama told my grandmama the part she lived through that my grandmama didn't live through and my grandmama told my mama what they both lived through and we were supposed to pass it down like that from generation so we'd never forget.

—Gayle Jones, American writer

Shrimp Jambalaya

2 onions, finely chopped
1 tablespoon butter
1 tablespoon flour
2 sprigs of thyme, chopped
2 sprigs of parsley, chopped
1 bay leaf
2 garlic cloves, finely minced
3 large tomatoes, finely chopped
1/2 teaspoon chili pepper
3 quarts broth, water or oyster liquid
80 lake shrimp, steamed, peeled, deveined
1 1/2 cups uncooked rice, rinsed, drained
salt and black pepper to taste
cayenne pepper to taste

Sauté the onions in the butter in a large saucepan until brown. Stir in the flour. Add the thyme, parsley, bay leaf and garlic and mix well. Sauté for 5 minutes or just until the garlic is tender but not brown.

Stir in the tomatoes with their juices and chili pepper. Simmer for 10 minutes, stirring occasionally. Add the broth and mix well. Bring to a boil. Boil for several minutes, stirring occasionally.

Add the shrimp. Cook for 5 minutes. Stir in the rice. Cook for 30 to 45 minutes or until the rice is tender, stirring occasionally.

Season with salt, black pepper and cayenne pepper. Serve immediately.

Serves eight to ten

Smothered Rabbit

2 rabbits, skinned, cleaned, cut into 6 pieces
1 cup flour
1 teaspoon salt
1/2 teaspoon black pepper
1/4 teaspoon thyme
1/2 cup butter
2 slices bacon
1 medium onion, sliced
4 sweet potatoes, peeled, sliced
2 potatoes, sliced
1 green bell pepper, sliced
4 carrots, sliced
2 cups water

Coat the rabbit with a mixture of the flour, salt, black pepper and thyme. Heat an iron skillet until hot. Add the butter. Heat until the butter is foamy. Add the bacon.

Fry the bacon just until light brown and remove to a plate. Add the rabbit to the skillet. Cook until brown on both sides.

Arrange the bacon, onion, sweet potatoes, potatoes, green pepper and carrots over the rabbit. Pour the water over the top.

Bake, covered, at 300 degrees for 45 minutes or until the vegetables are tender and the rabbit is cooked through.

Serves six

Corn Pudding

12 ears of corn
2 tablespoons butter
1 tablespoon sugar
4 egg yolks, beaten
4 cups milk
1/2 teaspoon salt
4 egg whites, stiffly beaten

Score the corn down each row of kernels. Scrape the kernels and starchy liquid into a bowl.

Combine the butter and sugar in a mixer bowl and mix well. Add the egg yolks, beating until smooth. Beat in the milk and salt. Mix in the corn. Fold in the egg whites.

Spoon the corn mixture into a baking dish. Cover with baking parchment. Bake at 350 degrees for 1 hour or until set.

Serves four to six

It's not so much about where you live; it's what's living in you. —Kweisi Mfume, American politician, social activist, and president of NAACP

Squash Casserole

2 pounds yellow squash, chopped
1 medium onion, chopped
1 tablespoon sugar
3 tablespoons melted butter
2 eggs, beaten
1 cup evaporated milk
1 teaspoon sage
salt and pepper to taste
2 cups cracker crumbs
2 cups shredded Cheddar cheese
paprika

Cook the squash in a small amount of water in a saucepan until tender; drain. Combine with the onion, sugar, butter, eggs, evaporated milk, sage, salt and pepper in a bowl and mix well. Add the cracker crumbs and half the cheese and mix well.

Spoon into a buttered 1½-quart baking dish. Sprinkle with the remaining 1 cup cheese and paprika. Bake at 350 degrees for 30 minutes or until bubbly.

Serves six

We raise de wheat, dey gib us de dorn;
We bake de bread, dey gib us de cruss;
We sif de meal, dey gib us de huss.
    —Antebellum African American humor

Succotash

2 cups shelled fresh lima beans
salt to taste
2 cups fresh or canned corn kernels
chopped onion to taste
chopped red bell pepper to taste
chopped green bell pepper to taste
1/3 cup cream or milk
1 tablespoon butter
1/2 teaspoon salt
1/8 teaspoon black pepper

Combine the lima beans and salt to taste with just enough water to cover in a saucepan. Simmer for 15 to 20 minutes or until tender, stirring occasionally.

Stir in the corn, onion, red pepper and green pepper. Simmer for 15 minutes or until most of the liquid has evaporated, stirring occasionally.

Stir in the cream, butter, 1/2 teaspoon salt and black pepper. Simmer just until heated through, stirring occasionally.

Serves four or five

Turnip and Mustard Greens

2 pounds fresh turnip greens and mustard greens
4 cups water
4 ounces ham hocks, salt pork, bacon, or hog jowls
salt to taste

Clean and rinse the greens. Combine the water and ham hocks in a large saucepan. Cook until the ham hocks are tender. Add the greens. Cook until the greens are tender, stirring occasionally. Drain, reserving 3 cups of the liquid.

Chop the greens fine and combine with the salt in a heated serving bowl; top with the ham hocks. Pour the reserved liquid over the top.

Do not add salt to the chopped greens if salt pork was used in the cooking. Serve with dumplings cooked in the reserved liquid if desired.

Serves four to six

Rice and Okra

3 slices bacon, chopped
2 cups cooked rice
1 cup cooked okra, cut into bite-size pieces

Fry the bacon in a skillet until crisp. Remove the bacon to a bowl. Add the rice and okra to the bacon drippings and mix well.

Simmer for several minutes, stirring occasionally. Stir in the bacon just before serving.

You may substitute 1 can of tomatoes for the okra.

Serves four

Hopping John

2 cups dried white peas or cowpeas
2 cups water
4 ounces chopped cooked ham
1 cup cooked rice
2 tablespoons butter
salt and pepper to taste

Sort and rinse the peas. Combine with enough water to cover in a bowl. Let stand for 8 to 10 hours; drain.

Combine the peas and 2 cups water in a saucepan. Cook until tender and only a small amount of water remains, stirring occasionally.

Stir the ham and rice into the peas. Add the butter, salt and pepper and mix well. Cook over low heat just until heated through, stirring occasionally.

Serve with roast pork and sweet potatoes.

Serves four to six

Especially do I believe in the Negro Race: in the beauty of its genius, the sweetness of its soul.
—W.E.B. DuBois, American sociologist and educator

Charleston Rice

1 onion, chopped
2 tablespoons butter
1 (14-ounce) can beef consommé
1 cup uncooked rice

Sauté the onion in the butter in a skillet. Add the consommé and rice. Pour into a 2-quart baking dish. Bake, covered, at 350 degrees for 1 hour or until the rice is tender.

Serves six

Hominy Grits

4 cups water
1 teaspoon salt
1 cup grits, rinsed
1 tablespoon butter

Bring the water and salt to a boil in a saucepan. Stir in the grits gradually. Cook, covered, over low heat for 30 to 40 minutes or until tender, stirring frequently.

Remove from the heat and stir in the butter. Serve immediately.

For variety, shape the warm grits into a log. Let stand until cool and cut into 1/2-inch slices. Dip the slices into beaten egg and coat with cornmeal. Fry in lard or bacon drippings until brown on both sides.

Serves four

Biscuits

2 cups flour
4 teaspoons baking powder
$1/2$ teaspoon salt
$1/4$ cup lard
1 teaspoon butter
water
milk

Sift the flour, baking powder and salt into a bowl and mix well. Cut in the lard and butter until crumbly. Add water and a small amount of milk to form a soft easily handled dough.

Pat the dough $1/2$ inch thick on a lightly floured surface; cut with a biscuit cutter.

Arrange the biscuits in a baking pan. Bake at 400 degrees until light brown.

Makes nine to twelve biscuits

Skillet Corn Bread

1 cup stone-ground white or yellow cornmeal
1 cup unbleached flour
1 tablespoon sugar
2 teaspoons baking powder
1/2 teaspoon salt
3/4 cup milk
2 tablespoons vegetable oil
1 egg, beaten

Mix the cornmeal, flour, sugar, baking powder and salt in a bowl. Whisk the milk, oil and egg in a bowl. Stir into the cornmeal mixture and mix well.

Spoon the batter into a lightly buttered or greased 9-inch cast-iron skillet or an 8x8-inch baking pan. Bake at 425 degrees for 25 to 30 minutes or until puffed and brown. Serve immediately.

Serves six

Crackling Bread

4 cups cornmeal
1 teaspoon salt
1/8 teaspoon baking soda
1 cup finely chopped cracklings
hot water

Mix the cornmeal, salt and baking soda in a bowl. Stir in the cracklings. Add just enough hot water to make a stiff batter and mix well.

Spoon the batter into a greased baking pan. Bake at 350 degrees until brown.

Serves six to eight

Hush Puppies

2 cups cornmeal
2 teaspoons baking powder
1 teaspoon salt
finely chopped onion to taste
2/3 cup milk
1 egg, slightly beaten
oil for deep-frying

Combine the cornmeal, baking powder, salt and onion in a bowl and mix well. Stir in the milk and egg. Shape into 1 1/2-inch balls. Deep-fry in hot oil until brown.

Hush puppies taste best when deep-fried in oil in which fish has been cooked.

Serves sixteen

There are two ways of exerting one's strength: One is pushing down, the other is pulling up.
—Booker T. Washington, American
educator, social reformer, and writer

Earnestine's Cream Cheese Pound Cake

3 cups sugar
8 ounces cream cheese, softened
1 cup butter, softened
1/2 cup margarine, softened
3 cups cake flour
6 eggs
2 teaspoons lemon extract
vanilla extract to taste

Beat the sugar, cream cheese, butter and margarine in a mixer bowl until light and fluffy, scraping the bowl occasionally. Add the cake flour alternately with the eggs, mixing well after each addition. Beat in the flavorings.

Spoon the batter into a greased and floured tube or bundt pan. Bake at 325 degrees for 1 1/2 hours or until the cake tests done. Cool in pan for 10 minutes. Invert onto a wire rack to cool completely.

Serves sixteen

To work with your hands is to feed your own mouth and maybe your neighbor's. To work with the mind is to unleash the feet of millions.
—Joseph Seamon Cotter, Sr., American poet and playwright

Earnestine's Lemon Buttermilk Pound Cake

1 teaspoon baking soda
1 tablespoon hot water
3 cups sugar
1 cup butter, softened
$1/2$ cup shortening
4 eggs
3 cups cake flour, sifted
1 cup buttermilk
1 tablespoon lemon extract
1 cup confectioners' sugar
$1/4$ cup lemon juice

Dissolve the baking soda in the hot water in a small bowl. Beat the sugar, butter and shortening in a mixer bowl until light and fluffy. Beat in the eggs 1 at a time.

Blend in the cake flour. Add the buttermilk, beating until smooth. Add the baking soda mixture and mix well. Beat in the flavoring.

Spoon the batter into a greased tube pan. Bake at 350 degrees for 1 hour. Invert onto a cake plate.

Drizzle the hot cake with a mixture of the confectioners' sugar and lemon juice.

Serves sixteen

One-Two-Three-Four Cup Cake

1 cup butter, softened
2 cups sugar
4 eggs, beaten
3 cups flour, sifted

Line the bottom of a round cake pan with baking parchment. Coat the paper lightly with butter.

Beat 1 cup butter in a mixer bowl until creamy. Add the sugar. Beat until light and fluffy, scraping the bowl occasionally.

Add the eggs gradually, beating constantly until blended. Add the flour and beat until blended, scraping the bowl occasionally.

Spoon the batter into the prepared cake pan. Bake at 350 degrees for 1 1/4 hours or until the cake tests done.

This unleavened cake was popular in plantation cooking.

Serves six to eight

When you clench your fist, no one can put anything in your hand, nor can your hand pick anything up.
—Alex Haley

Earnestine's Chocolate Chip Cookie Pie

2 eggs
1/2 cup flour
1/2 cup sugar
1/2 cup packed brown sugar
1/2 cup melted butter, cooled
1 cup chocolate chips
1 cup chopped walnuts or pecans
1 unbaked (9-inch) pie shell
whipped cream (optional)

Beat the eggs in a mixer bowl until foamy. Add the flour, sugar and brown sugar and beat until blended. Add the butter, beating until smooth. Stir in the chocolate chips and walnuts.

Spoon the mixture into the pie shell. Bake at 325 degrees for 1 hour. Let stand until cool. Spread with whipped cream.

Serves six

Earnestine's Egg Pie

    1 cup sugar
    3 egg yolks
    3/4 cup butter, softened
    3 tablespoons flour
    1 (12-ounce) can evaporated milk
    1 teaspoon vanilla extract
    1/2 teaspoon nutmeg
    1 unbaked (9-inch) pie shell

Beat the sugar and egg yolks in a mixer bowl until creamy, scraping the bowl occasionally. Add the butter and flour. Beat until blended. Beat in the evaporated milk, vanilla and nutmeg.

Spoon the mixture into the pie shell. Bake at 300 degrees for 50 minutes or until set.

Serves six

What is soul? It's like electricity—we don't really know what it is, but it's a force that can light a room.
                        —Ray Charles, American musician and composer

Fried Pies

1 pound fruit of choice, peeled, sliced
1/2 cup sugar
1 tablespoon cornstarch
1/8 teaspoon spice to complement fruit used
2 cups flour
1 teaspoon salt
1/2 cup shortening
1/2 cup ice water
vegetable oil for frying

Combine the fruit with just enough water to cover in a saucepan. Bring to a boil and cook until the fruit is tender and most of the liquid has been absorbed, stirring occasionally. Stir in the sugar, cornstarch and spice.

Mix the flour and salt in a bowl. Cut in the shortening until crumbly. Add the ice water 1 tablespoon at a time, mixing with a fork until the mixture forms a ball.

Roll the dough 1/16 inch thick on a lightly floured surface. Cut into twelve 5-inch circles.

Spoon some of the fruit into the center of each circle. Moisten the edges with water and fold the circles to enclose the filling. Press the edges with a fork to seal.

Add oil to a deep-fat fryer or electric skillet to a depth of 2 to 3 inches. Heat to 365 degrees. Fry the pies in the hot oil for 3 minutes or until golden brown, turning once. Remove with a slotted spoon; drain. Serve warm or at room temperature.

Makes twelve fried pies

Sweet Potato Pie

2 cups mashed cooked sweet potatoes
1 cup sugar
$1/2$ cup melted butter
$1/3$ cup milk
2 eggs, beaten
1 teaspoon nutmeg
$1/2$ teaspoon baking powder
1 teaspoon vanilla extract
$1/8$ teaspoon salt
1 unbaked (8-inch) pie shell

Combine the sweet potatoes, sugar, butter, milk, eggs, nutmeg, baking powder, vanilla and salt in a bowl and mix well.

Spoon the mixture into the pie shell. Bake at 425 degrees until the pie tests done.

Serves six

Presumption should never make us neglect that which appears easy to us, nor despair make us lose courage at the sight of difficulties.

—Benjamin Banneker, American mathematician, social activist, and astronomer

Benne Seed Wafers

1 cup packed brown sugar
1/4 cup butter
1 egg, beaten
1/2 cup flour
1/4 teaspoon salt
1/8 teaspoon baking powder
1 cup sesame seeds (benne seeds), toasted
1 teaspoon lemon juice
1/2 teaspoon vanilla extract

Beat the brown sugar and butter in a mixer bowl until creamy, scraping the bowl occasionally. Stir in the egg, flour, salt and baking powder. Add the sesame seeds, lemon juice and vanilla and mix well.

Drop by teaspoonfuls 2 inches apart onto a greased baking sheet. Bake at 325 degrees for 15 minutes or until brown around the edges. Cool on baking sheet for 2 minutes. Remove to a wire rack to cool completely.

Makes twelve to sixteen wafers

America is not like a blanket—one piece of
unbroken cloth, the same color, the same texture,
the same size. America is more like a quilt—
many patches, many pieces, many colors,
many sizes, all woven and held together by
a common thread. —Jesse Jackson

The same struggle that preserved the unity of the states
made Africans citizens of that union. The union demonstrates, in all
its imperfection, that north and south, black and white, rich and poor,
like the two-headed crocodile, share one destiny and should work
together toward it.

The melting pot of America is truly found in its kitchens,
and although much of the contribution of African cuisine has been
unrecognized, it has long been felt, from gumbo and dirty rice to
turnip greens and corn bread dressing.

African Americans
An Imperfect Union

FUNTUMMIREKU-DƐNKYƐMMIREKU
(Fun-tum-me-rek-koo - Den-chim-me-rek-koo)

Two-headed crocodile with
a common stomach

FUNTUMMIREKU-DƐNKYƐMMIREKU is the symbol of democracy, unity in diversity,
or the oneness of the human family despite cultural differences and diversities.

Mini Quiches

2 tablespoons grated onion
2 ounces bacon, chopped
2 tablespoons butter
1 cup half-and-half
2 eggs, beaten
1/2 teaspoon salt
1/8 teaspoon nutmeg
1/8 teaspoon pepper
1/2 cup shredded Swiss cheese
12 small pastry shells

Sauté the onion and bacon in the butter in a skillet until the bacon is crisp.

Whisk the half-and-half, eggs, salt, nutmeg and pepper in a bowl. Stir in the bacon mixture and cheese.

Spoon into the pastry shells. Bake at 350 degrees until set.

Makes twelve appetizer quiches

Let us refrain from doing evil to each other, and let us love each other as brothers, as we are the same flesh and blood....It is a fool who does not love himself and his people.
—Elijah Muhammad, American religious leader

Navy Bean Soup with Ham Hocks

3 pounds dried navy beans
3 medium onions, minced
3 ribs celery, chopped
5 garlic cloves, minced
1/4 cup olive oil
2 smoked ham hocks
4 quarts water
1 (6-ounce) can tomato paste
1 cup chopped fresh parsley, or 1/2 cup parsley flakes
3 carrots, cut into 1/8-inch slices
2 tablespoons fresh minced marjoram,
   or 1 tablespoon dried marjoram
1 tablespoon salt
pepper to taste

Sort and rinse the beans. Combine with enough water to cover in a bowl.
Let stand for 8 to 10 hours; drain.

Cook the onions, celery and garlic in the olive oil in a stockpot over
medium heat for 15 minutes or until tender, stirring frequently. Add the navy
beans, ham hocks and 4 quarts water.

Stir in the tomato paste, parsley, carrots, marjoram, salt and pepper.
Bring to a boil and reduce the heat. Simmer, covered, for several hours or
until the beans are very tender and the soup is of the desired consistency.

Serves twenty-four

Ambrosia Salad

1 (11-ounce) can mandarin oranges, drained
1 (6-ounce) can pineapple chunks, drained, chopped
1 cup shredded coconut
1 cup miniature marshmallows
1 tablespoon chopped nuts
1 cup sour cream

Combine the oranges, pineapple, coconut, marshmallows and nuts in a bowl and mix well. Chill, covered, for 1 hour. Stir in the sour cream just before serving.

Serves four

Corn Salad

2 (16-ounce) cans whole kernel corn, drained
4 plum tomatoes, thinly sliced
1 unpeeled cucumber, thinly sliced
1/2 cup chopped green bell pepper
1/2 cup chopped red bell pepper
2 green onions, chopped
salt and freshly ground black pepper to taste
1/3 (8-ounce) bottle (or more) Russian salad dressing

Combine the corn, tomatoes, cucumber, green pepper, red pepper and green onions in a bowl and mix gently. Season with salt and black pepper. Add about 1/3 of the salad dressing and mix well. Chill, covered, for 1 hour before serving.

Serve as a salad with grilled meat, fish or poultry or over salad greens as the main course with soft garlic bread sticks.

Serves eight

Stuffed Bell Peppers

1 medium onion, finely chopped
1 rib celery, finely chopped
4 sprigs of parsley, finely chopped
1/2 teaspoon thyme
1 cup butter
8 ounces ground beef, twice-ground
8 ounces small shrimp, peeled, deveined
1/2 loaf dry French bread
3 eggs, beaten
1 teaspoon garlic powder
salt and black pepper to taste
3 large green bell peppers
1/2 cup bread crumbs
melted butter

Sauté the onion, celery, parsley and thyme in 1 cup butter in a skillet for 10 to 15 minutes. Stir in the ground beef and shrimp.

Soak the French bread in water in a bowl just until moist; drain and squeeze out the excess moisture. Combine with the eggs. Stir in the ground beef mixture. Add the garlic powder, salt and black pepper and mix well. Spoon into a baking dish.

Bake at 350 degrees for 1 1/2 hours. Chill, covered, in the refrigerator. Skim the fat from top.

Cut the green peppers into halves horizontally, discarding the seeds and membranes. Blanch in boiling water in a saucepan for 2 minutes; drain.

Spoon the mixture into the bell pepper halves. Arrange on a baking sheet. Sprinkle with the bread crumbs and drizzle with melted butter. Broil for 15 to 20 minutes or until heated through.

Serves six

Texas Chili

1 (15-ounce) can peeled tomatoes
3 pounds ground or cubed sirloin steak
1 large white onion, chopped
pork drippings
1 large garlic clove, chopped
1 tablespoon garlic powder
1 (15-ounce) can tomato sauce
1 cup catsup
6 red chile peppers, chopped (optional)
6 tablespoons (heaping) chili powder
3 tablespoons (or more) salt
2 tablespoons cayenne pepper
2 tablespoons cumin
1 tablespoon black pepper
1 tablespoon oregano
1 tablespoon Tabasco sauce
flour or filé powder (optional)

Drain and chop the tomatoes, reserving the juice. Sauté the ground steak and onion in pork drippings in a skillet until the beef is cooked through; drain.

Stir in the garlic and garlic powder. Add the tomato sauce and tomatoes and mix well. Simmer until heated through, stirring and adding the reserved juice if needed to cover the meat. Add the catsup, chile peppers, chili powder, salt, cayenne pepper, cumin, black pepper, oregano and Tabasco sauce 1 ingredient at a time, mixing well after each addition.

Simmer for 1 1/2 hours or longer, stirring frequently, adding flour or filé powder if needed for the desired consistency.

Serves eight to ten

Glazed Ham

1 (8- to 10-pound) ham
pineapple slices
maraschino cherries
whole cloves
1½ cups packed dark brown sugar
½ cup rum
¼ cup orange juice

Preheat the oven to 450 degrees. Score the ham and arrange in a baking pan. Reduce the oven temperature to 325 degrees. Bake the ham for 20 minutes per pound. Increase the oven temperature to 425 degrees.

Remove the ham from the oven and arrange the pineapple slices, maraschino cherries and cloves in a decorative pattern over the top.

Mix the brown sugar, rum and orange juice in a bowl. Drizzle over the ham. Bake until the glaze caramelizes.

Serves fifteen to twenty

Chopped Barbecue

3 pounds bone-in pork shoulder roast
2 tablespoons crushed red pepper flakes
2 teaspoons salt
1 teaspoon freshly ground black pepper
1/2 to 1 cup white vinegar
2 medium onions, finely chopped
1 green bell pepper, chopped
2 cups barbecue sauce

Rinse the pork roast and pat dry. Rub with a mixture of the red pepper flakes, salt and black pepper. Marinate in the refrigerator, covered loosely with waxed paper, for 8 to 10 hours.

Place the roast in a shallow roasting pan. Let stand at room temperature for 1 hour. Pour the desired amount of vinegar over the roast. Sprinkle the onions and green pepper in the pan.

Roast until a meat thermometer inserted in the thickest portion of the roast registers 180 degrees, basting with the pan juices several times. Let stand for 1 hour.

Chop the pork, reserving the pan juices. Combine with the reserved pan juices and barbecue sauce in a saucepan. Cook until heated through. Serve with potato salad and coleslaw.

Serves eight

Basic Barbecue Sauce

1 cup catsup
¼ cup cider vinegar or red wine vinegar
3 tablespoons brown sugar
2 garlic cloves, minced
1 tablespoon dry or prepared mustard
1 teaspoon Worcestershire sauce
½ teaspoon cayenne pepper or Tabasco sauce
½ yellow onion, finely chopped (optional)

Combine the catsup, cider vinegar, brown sugar, garlic, mustard, Worcestershire sauce and cayenne pepper in a saucepan and mix well. Bring to a boil and reduce the heat to low.

Cook for 5 minutes or until thickened, stirring frequently. Adjust flavor by adding the onion or additional vinegar, brown sugar and/or cayenne pepper to suit your taste.

Store, covered, in the refrigerator for 1 week before using to enhance flavors. Store in the refrigerator for up to 1 month.

Makes one and one-fourth cups

All-Purpose Seasoning Rub

1 teaspoon salt
1 teaspoon ground black pepper
1 teaspoon paprika
1 teaspoon cayenne pepper
2 garlic cloves, minced, or 1 tablespoon garlic powder
¼ cup vegetable oil

Mix the salt, black pepper, paprika, cayenne pepper, garlic and oil in a bowl. Store in a jar with a tightfitting lid for several months. Add the oil just before using.

Use as a rub for beef, chicken, pork or fish. Marinate beef or chicken, covered with plastic wrap, in the refrigerator for 8 to 10 hours and fish for 30 to 60 minutes. Bake or grill as desired.

Makes one-third cup

You can give a man some food and he'll eat it. Then he'll be hungry again. But give a man some ground and he'll never be hungry no more.
—Fannie Lou Hamer, activist and founder of the Mississippi Freedom Democratic Party

Camille O. Cosby's Satisfying Stewed Chicken

1 (2½- to 3-pound) chicken, cut up
1 medium onion, chopped
2 or 3 tomatoes, chopped, or 1 (8-ounce) can tomatoes
juice of 1 lemon
1 teaspoon cumin
½ teaspoon chopped fresh oregano
chopped gingerroot to taste
8 ounces fresh okra, sliced
salt to taste
hot cooked brown rice

Brown the chicken on all sides in a nonstick skillet. Add the onion. Cook until the onion is translucent.

Stir in the tomatoes, lemon juice, cumin, oregano and gingerroot. Simmer for 30 minutes, stirring occasionally. Add the okra and mix well. Simmer for 10 to 15 minutes longer or until the chicken is cooked through. Season with salt.

Serve over brown rice with a tossed green salad and flat bread.

Serves four or five

Hearty Corn Bread Chicken Pie

3 chicken breasts
1/2 cup finely chopped Vidalia onion
1/2 cup chopped green bell pepper
1/2 cup chopped red bell pepper
1/2 cup butter
1/4 cup flour
1 teaspoon salt
1/2 teaspoon oregano
2 cups whole milk or evaporated milk
1/2 cup drained Mexicorn
1/2 cup green peas
1/2 cup cornmeal
1/2 cup flour
1 1/2 teaspoons baking powder
1/2 teaspoon salt
2/3 cup milk
3 tablespoons melted butter
1 egg, beaten
4 ounces sharp Cheddar cheese, shredded
melted butter

Combine the chicken with just enough water to cover in a saucepan. Simmer for 10 to 18 minutes or just until tender; do not overcook. Drain, reserving 1/2 cup of the broth. Chop the chicken into bite-size pieces.

Sauté the onion, green pepper and red pepper in 1/2 cup butter in a skillet over medium heat just until tender. Stir in 1/4 cup flour. Cook for 1 minute. Mix in 1 teaspoon salt and oregano.

Add the reserved chicken broth, 2 cups milk, corn and peas and mix well. Cook until the mixture begins to thicken, stirring frequently. Stir in the chicken. Spoon into a round baking dish.

Mix the cornmeal, 1/2 cup flour, baking powder and 1/2 teaspoon salt in a bowl. Add 2/3 cup milk, 3 tablespoons butter and egg and mix well. Stir in the cheese. Spoon over the chicken mixture.

Bake at 425 degrees for 20 to 25 minutes or until golden brown. Brush with melted butter.

Serves four to six

Salmon Croquettes

1 pound cooked fresh or canned salmon
1/2 yellow onion, chopped
1/2 cup mashed potatoes
1/4 cup finely chopped fresh parsley
2 eggs, beaten
salt and ground pepper to taste
1/4 cup flour
3 to 4 tablespoons vegetable oil

Flake the salmon in a bowl, discarding any bones. Stir in the onion, mashed potatoes, parsley, eggs, salt and pepper. Shape into 3-inch patties, 1/2 inch thick. Coat with a mixture of the flour, salt and pepper.

Fry the patties in the oil in a skillet over medium-high heat for 3 to 4 minutes on each side or until brown, turning once. Serve immediately.

Serves four

Can't tell much about a chicken pie till you get through de crust. —Anonymous

Crab Cakes

1/4 cup finely minced yellow onion
1/4 cup finely minced celery
1 teaspoon finely minced garlic
2 tablespoons melted butter
1 cup whipping cream
1/8 teaspoon crushed red pepper
1/2 teaspoon ground black pepper
1/4 teaspoon kosher salt
1 1/2 pounds Dungeness 60/40 crab meat blend
1/4 cup mayonnaise
1 tablespoon Dijon mustard
1 cup bread crumbs
melted butter

Sauté the onion, celery and garlic in 2 tablespoons butter in a skillet. Stir in the whipping cream, red pepper, black pepper and salt. Cook until thickened, stirring frequently. Cool for 15 to 20 minutes.

Squeeze the moisture from the crab meat. Combine with the cream mixture, mayonnaise and Dijon mustard in a bowl. Mix in 1/2 cup of the bread crumbs. Shape into 2-ounce balls; flatten to 1/2 inch thickness. Coat with the remaining 1/2 cup bread crumbs.

Fry the patties in melted butter in a skillet until brown on all sides. Serve with Roasted Pepper Pesto (page 121).

Serves four to six

Roasted Pepper Pesto

1 red bell pepper
1 yellow bell pepper
1 green bell pepper
vegetable oil
$1/4$ cup pine nuts, toasted
$1/4$ cup virgin olive oil
2 tablespoons minced fresh basil leaves

Coat the bell peppers lightly with vegetable oil. Arrange on a baking sheet. Roast at 400 degrees for 15 to 20 minutes, turning frequently. Remove to a bowl and let stand, covered with plastic wrap, until cool. Peel, seed and chop the bell peppers.

Combine the bell peppers, pine nuts, olive oil and basil in a food processor container. Process until minced.

Makes three cups

The task that remains is to cope with our interdependence—to see ourselves reflected in every other human being and to respect and honor our differences.

—Melba Patillo Beals, American author,
member of the Little Rock Nine

Seafood Gumbo

2 quarts beef stock or canned beef broth
1 cup chopped smoked ham
2 bay leaves
2 tablespoons crushed red pepper flakes
2 teaspoons salt
1/3 cup bacon drippings
1/3 cup flour
3 cups chopped fresh or thawed frozen okra
2 large onions, chopped
1 green bell pepper, minced
2 ribs celery, chopped
2 garlic cloves, minced
3 tablespoons vegetable oil
1 (16-ounce) can whole tomatoes
1/4 cup catsup
1 tablespoon hot pepper sauce
1 tablespoon Worcestershire sauce
1 teaspoon salt
1/2 teaspoon thyme
1 pound shrimp, peeled, deveined
1 pound crab meat
1 bunch scallions, chopped
12 shucked fresh oysters with liquid
1 cup cooked rice
1 tablespoon filé powder
hot cooked rice

Combine the beef stock, ham, bay leaves, red pepper flakes and
2 teaspoons salt in a stockpot. Bring to a boil over high heat and reduce the
heat. Simmer, covered, for 1 hour, stirring occasionally.

Heat the bacon drippings in a skillet over medium heat. Blend in the
flour. Cook over low heat for 25 minutes or until the flour turns dark brown
and the roux smells nutty, stirring constantly.

Sauté the okra, onions, green pepper, celery and garlic in the oil in a
separate skillet over medium heat for 10 minutes or until tender-crisp. Add
the tomatoes and mix well. Cook for 5 minutes longer, stirring frequently.

Stir the roux and sautéed vegetables into the hot stock mixture. Add the catsup, hot pepper sauce, Worcestershire sauce, 1 teaspoon salt and thyme. Simmer, covered, for 1 hour, stirring occasionally. The dish may be prepared to this point 1 day in advance and stored, covered, in the refrigerator until just before adding the remaining ingredients.

Add the shrimp, crab meat and scallions and mix well. Cook for 10 minutes, stirring occasionally. Stir in the oysters, 1 cup rice and filé powder. Cook for 10 minutes, stirring occasionally. Discard the bay leaves. Adjust the seasonings. Spoon over additional hot cooked rice in bowls.

You may substitute 6 hard-shell cleaned cooked crabs for the crab meat and one 12-ounce jar drained oysters for the fresh oysters.

Serves six to eight

We cannot think of uniting with others, until after we have first united among ourselves. We cannot think of being acceptable to others until we have first proven acceptable to ourselves. —Malcolm X, American cleric, activist

Crab Quiche

1 unbaked (10-inch) deep-dish pie shell
8 ounces crab meat, shrimp or broccoli
4 ounces Swiss cheese, shredded
4 ounces Gruyère cheese, grated
1 tablespoon flour
2 eggs, at room temperature
1 cup half-and-half
1 teaspoon MSG (optional)
3/4 teaspoon salt
1/8 teaspoon pepper
1/8 teaspoon Tabasco sauce

Bake the pie shell for 10 minutes using the package directions. Mix the crab meat, Swiss cheese, Gruyère cheese and flour in a bowl. Spread evenly in the pie shell.

Whisk the eggs in a bowl until foamy. Add the half-and-half, MSG, salt, pepper and Tabasco sauce and mix well. Pour over the crab meat mixture.

Bake at 325 degrees for 1 hour or until set. Cut into wedges to serve.

Serves six

Black-Eyed Peas

1 pound dried black-eyed peas
2 or 3 large ham hocks
1 rib celery, chopped
1 onion, chopped
1 bay leaf
salt and pepper to taste

Sort and rinse the peas. Combine with enough cold water to cover in a bowl. Let stand for 20 minutes; drain.

Combine the peas, ham hocks, celery, onion, bay leaf, salt and pepper in a large saucepan. Add enough cold water to cover by 1 inch.

Simmer, covered, for 2 hours or until the peas are tender but not mushy, stirring occasionally and adding additional water as needed. Discard the bay leaf.

You may substitute 2 smoked turkey legs or wings for the ham hocks if preferred.

Serves six

Fried Okra

1 cup cornmeal
1 teaspoon paprika
1/2 teaspoon salt
1/4 teaspoon ground pepper
1 pound okra, cut into 1/2-inch slices
1/4 cup vegetable oil

Combine the cornmeal, paprika, salt and pepper in a bowl or sealable plastic bag. Add the okra in batches and shake or toss until coated.

Heat the oil in a cast-iron skillet over high heat. Fry the okra in the hot oil for 5 to 7 minutes or until golden brown. Remove with a slotted spoon to paper towels to drain. Serve immediately.

Serves four

Fried Green Tomatoes

 3 green tomatoes
 1/2 cup cornmeal
 1 teaspoon paprika
 1 teaspoon flour
 3/4 teaspoon salt
 3/4 teaspoon ground pepper
 1/4 cup vegetable oil

Cut the tomatoes horizontally into thick slices. Mix the cornmeal, paprika, flour, salt and pepper in a shallow dish. Coat the tomato slices with the cornmeal mixture and arrange in a single layer on a baking sheet. Place in the freezer for 5 minutes or in the refrigerator for 20 minutes to allow the coating to absorb the moisture from the tomatoes.

Heat the oil in a nonstick skillet over medium-high heat. Coat the tomato slices again with the remaining cornmeal mixture. Fry in the hot oil for 3 minutes on each side or until brown; drain. Serve immediately.

Serves six

Mashed Turnips

 5 pounds turnips, peeled, chopped
 3 quarts water
 2 tablespoons butter
 2 tablespoons evaporated skim milk
 1 tablespoon sugar
 1 tablespoon freshly ground pepper
 1 teaspoon salt

Cook the turnips in the water in a saucepan until tender; drain.

Mash the turnips with the butter, evaporated skim milk, sugar, pepper and salt in a bowl.

Serves eight

Wild Mushroom Ragout with Grits

½ cup finely chopped white onion
½ cup finely chopped elephant garlic
½ cup finely chopped celery
½ cup finely chopped carrot
½ cup finely chopped green and red bell pepper
½ cup butter
1 pound fresh shiitake mushrooms, thickly sliced
1 pound fresh domestic mushrooms, thickly sliced
1 pound fresh oyster mushrooms, thickly sliced
1 tablespoon chopped wild thyme
1 tablespoon chopped fresh rosemary
1 tablespoon chopped fresh basil
¼ cup sherry
¼ cup olive oil
½ cup flour
4 cups chicken stock
quick-cooking grits

Sauté the onion, garlic, celery, carrot and bell pepper in the butter in a skillet until wilted.

Add the mushrooms and mix well. Sauté until the mushrooms are wilted. Stir in the thyme, rosemary and basil. Sauté until wilted.

Add the sherry and mix well. Simmer for 10 minutes, stirring occasionally.

Heat the olive oil in a skillet. Blend in the flour. Cook until the roux is dark brown in color, stirring constantly. Add the roux to the mushroom mixture and mix well. Stir in the stock. Bring to a light boil and reduce the heat.

Simmer for 30 minutes, stirring occasionally. Add a mixture of cornstarch and water if the ragout appears too thin. Spoon into a greased 9x13-inch baking dish.

Prepare the grits using the package directions. Spoon over the mushroom layer. Bake at 350 degrees for 30 minutes or until set.

Serves four to six

Dirty Rice

1/2 red onion, finely chopped
1/2 red bell pepper, finely chopped
1/2 green bell pepper, finely chopped
2 tablespoons vegetable oil
1 or 2 chicken livers, chopped
2 green onions with tops, chopped
2 garlic cloves, minced
1 teaspoon thyme, crushed
1/2 teaspoon paprika
1/4 teaspoon allspice
1/4 teaspoon ground mace (optional)
1/8 to 1/2 teaspoon cayenne pepper
1/4 teaspoon sugar
1 bay leaf
1/4 cup water or chicken stock
salt and black pepper to taste
2 cups hot cooked rice

Sauté the onion, red pepper and green pepper in the oil in a 10-inch skillet for 5 minutes or until tender. Stir in the chicken livers, green onions and garlic. Cook for 1 minute, stirring frequently.

Add the thyme, paprika, allspice, mace, cayenne pepper, sugar and bay leaf. Cook for 30 seconds, stirring constantly. Stir in the water. Season with salt and black pepper. Add the rice and mix well.

Cook just until heated through, stirring frequently. Discard the bay leaf. Adjust the seasonings.

Serves four

Corn Bread Dressing

  6 cups cubed corn bread
  1 yellow onion, chopped
  1 green bell pepper, chopped
  2 ribs celery, chopped
  1/2 cup butter
  2 teaspoons sage
  1 1/2 teaspoons thyme
  salt and black pepper to taste
  1 to 1 1/2 cups Chicken or Turkey stock

Mix the corn bread, onion, green pepper, celery, butter, sage, thyme, salt and black pepper in a bowl. Add enough stock to moisten as desired and mix well.

Spoon the mixture into a buttered 4-quart baking dish. Bake, covered, at 375 degrees for 30 minutes. Bake, uncovered, for 30 minutes longer or until brown. Decrease the amount of liquid added if used as a stuffing for a turkey.

Chicken or Turkey Stock

  chicken or turkey wing tips, neck, liver and/or gizzard
  celery tops
  chopped onion
  bay leaf
  4 cups water

Combine the chicken or turkey parts, celery tops, onion, bay leaf and water in a large saucepan. Bring to a boil and reduce the heat. Simmer for 40 to 60 minutes.

Strain, reserving the liquid, liver and gizzard. Chop the liver and gizzard and add to the dressing mixture if desired. Use the stock to prepare the dressing and gravy.

The stock may be stored, covered, in the refrigerator for up to 5 days or in the freezer for up to 6 months.

Serves six to eight

Rice and Peas

2 cups dried black-eyed peas
4 ounces salt pork, chopped
4 cups water
salt to taste
2 cups uncooked rice, rinsed
1 large tomato, crushed
1 tablespoon lime juice
1 tablespoon butter
chopped fresh herbs to taste

Sort and rinse the peas. Combine with the salt pork, water and salt in a saucepan. Cook for 20 minutes, stirring occasionally.

Add the rice, tomato, lime juice, butter and herbs and mix well.

Cook, covered, over medium heat for 5 to 7 minutes; reduce the heat. Cook over low heat for 30 minutes or until all of the water is absorbed and the rice and peas are tender. Serve immediately.

Serves four

To that which is deepest and truest in the common traditions that unite Americans, and it tells us that despite the temporary problems of the moment, the Dream is still working in us and through us and that the darkness is still light enough.

—John H. Johnson, American publisher

Macaroni and Cheese

1 cup uncooked elbow macaroni
1/2 cup evaporated milk
1/2 cup water
1 egg
2 teaspoons salt
1/4 cup margarine
2 cups shredded Cheddar cheese

Cook the macaroni using the package directions. Rinse and drain.

Whisk the evaporated milk and water in a bowl. Add the egg, whisking until blended. Stir in the salt.

Stir in the macaroni. Let stand for 1 minute. Add whole milk or additional skim milk if the macaroni absorbs all of the milk mixture.

Layer the macaroni, margarine and cheese 1/2 at a time in a greased baking dish. Bake at 350 degrees for 25 to 30 minutes or until bubbly. Serve immediately.

Serves four to six

Banana Bread

2 cups flour
1 teaspoon baking soda
1 teaspoon cinnamon
1/2 teaspoon salt
1 cup sugar
4 ounces cream cheese, softened (optional)
1/2 cup butter, softened
2 eggs
4 large ripe bananas, mashed
1 tablespoon vanilla extract
2 cups chopped walnuts (optional)
1/4 cup milk

Sift the flour, baking soda, cinnamon and salt into a bowl and mix well.
Beat the sugar, cream cheese and butter in a mixer bowl until creamy.
Beat in the eggs 1 at a time. Mix in the bananas and vanilla.

Combine the walnuts and milk in a bowl and mix well. Stir into the
banana mixture. Add the flour mixture 1 cup at a time, mixing just
until blended.

Spoon the batter into a buttered 5x9-inch loaf pan. Bake at 325 degrees
for 1 hour or until the loaf tests done. Cool in the pan for several minutes.
Remove to a wire rack to cool completely.

Makes one loaf

Sweet Potato Angel Biscuits

1 envelope dry yeast
1/4 cup warm (105- to 115-degree) water
1 tablespoon sugar
2 cups baking mix
3/4 cup mashed cooked sweet potatoes

Dissolve the yeast in the water in a medium bowl. Stir in the sugar. Add the baking mix and sweet potatoes, stirring to form a soft dough.

Turn the dough onto a hard surface dusted lightly with additional baking mix and shape into a ball. Knead 10 times. Roll 1/2 inch thick; cut with a 2-inch cutter dipped in additional baking mix.

Arrange the rounds on an ungreased baking sheet. Let rise in a warm place for 30 minutes or until puffed and light. Bake at 425 degrees for 6 to 8 minutes or until golden brown.

Makes fifteen biscuits

We have flown the air like birds and swum the sea like fishers, but have yet to learn the simple act of walking the earth like brothers.

—Martin Luther King, Jr., American cleric, civil
rights leader, and writer

Earnestine's Broccoli Bread

1 (9-ounce) package corn bread mix
1 (10-ounce) package frozen chopped broccoli
1 cup cottage cheese
4 eggs, beaten
1 large onion, chopped (optional)
1 to 2 tablespoons margarine

Combine the corn bread mix, broccoli, cottage cheese, eggs and onion in a bowl and mix well.

Heat the margarine in a 9x13-inch baking dish until melted, tilting the dish to coat the bottom and sides. Spoon the corn bread mixture into the prepared dish. Bake at 350 degrees until golden brown.

Serves six to eight

In our racial and ethnic diversity, we are all brothers and sisters in a quest for greatness.
—Harold Washington, American politician

Corn Bread

 1½ cups white or yellow cornmeal
 1½ cups unbleached flour
 1 tablespoon sugar (optional)
 1 tablespoon baking powder
 ½ teaspoon salt
 1 egg
 ½ cup safflower oil, corn oil or canola oil
 1½ cups milk or buttermilk

Mix the cornmeal, flour, sugar, baking powder and salt in a bowl. Whisk the egg in a bowl. Stir in the safflower oil and milk. Add to the cornmeal mixture, stirring just until moistened.

Spoon the cornmeal mixture into a greased 10-inch ovenproof skillet. Bake at 400 degrees for 40 to 50 minutes or just until the top begins to brown. Serve immediately.

You may also cook in an 8x8-inch baking pan, 10-inch cake pan or 10 muffin cups. Decrease the baking time to 20 to 25 minutes for the muffins.

Serves ten

Baking Powder Dumplings

1 cup flour
2 teaspoons baking powder
1/2 teaspoon salt
1/2 cup milk
chicken broth

Mix the flour, baking powder and salt in a bowl. Stir in the milk. Beat with an electric mixer or wooden spoon to form a stiff dough.

Bring the chicken broth to a boil in a saucepan. Drop the dough by teaspoonfuls into the boiling broth. Cook, covered, for 10 to 15 minutes or until the dumplings are tender and puffed.

Serves four to six

Deal with yourself as an individual worthy of respect, and make everyone else deal with you the same way.
—Nikki Giovanni, poet

Baked Apples

8 firm apples
1 tablespoon cinnamon
2 teaspoons nutmeg
1/2 cup raisins
3/4 cup water

Rinse and core the apples, leaving the bases intact; cut a thin slice from the top of each. Arrange the apples cut side up in a baking dish. Sprinkle with the cinnamon and nutmeg. Spoon the raisins into the cavities.

Pour the water around the apples. Bake at 400 degrees for 30 to 35 minutes or until they are easily pricked with a fork but still hold their shape, basting with the pan juices every 15 minutes.

Serve warm or cold topped with cream, yogurt or whipped topping sprinkled with additional cinnamon.

You may substitute whole cranberry sauce, crushed peppermint candy, chopped nuts or granola for the raisins.

Serves eight

Banana Pudding

1 1/2 cups sugar
1/2 cup plus 2 tablespoons flour
5 cups milk
5 egg yolks, beaten
2 1/2 teaspoons vanilla extract
49 vanilla wafers
7 bananas, sliced
5 egg whites
1/2 teaspoon salt
1/2 teaspoon cream of tartar
1/2 cup sugar

Mix 1 1/2 cups sugar and flour in a saucepan. Add the milk gradually, stirring constantly. Cook over medium heat for 30 minutes or until thick and creamy, stirring constantly.

Stir 2 cups of the hot pudding mixture into the egg yolks. Stir the egg yolk mixture into the pudding mixture.

Cook for 5 minutes longer, stirring constantly. Remove from the heat. Stir in the vanilla. Let stand for 30 minutes.

Layer the vanilla wafers, bananas and pudding alternately in an ovenproof dish or bowl until all of the ingredients are used, ending with the pudding.

Beat the egg whites, salt and cream of tartar in a mixer bowl until foamy. Add 1/2 cup sugar gradually, beating constantly until stiff peaks form. Spread over the prepared layers sealing to the edges. Bake at 250 degrees until light brown. Chill until serving time.

Serves six to eight

Bread Pudding

3 cups milk
3/4 cup sugar
1/2 cup melted butter
4 eggs, beaten
1 tablespoon vanilla extract
1/2 teaspoon freshly grated nutmeg
1/2 teaspoon cinnamon
10 slices dried wheat bread or
    French bread, lightly toasted, cubed
3/4 cup golden raisins or currants

Whisk the milk, sugar, butter, eggs, vanilla, nutmeg and cinnamon in a bowl until blended. Stir in the bread cubes and raisins. Pour into a buttered 9x13-inch baking dish.

Bake at 325 degrees for 40 to 50 minutes or until a knife inserted in the center comes out clean. Serve hot.

You may substitute 1 to 2 cups blueberries, 2 grated apples, an 8-ounce can drained crushed pineapple, an 8-ounce can drained fruit cocktail, an 8-ounce can drained canned peaches or a 20-ounce can drained jackfruit for the raisins. Substitute a mixture of one 12-ounce can evaporated milk and 1 cup water for the whole milk for an old-fashioned flavor.

Serves eight to ten

Chocolate Intrigue Cake

3 cups sifted flour
2 teaspoons baking powder
$1/2$ teaspoon salt
1 cup milk
$1^{1}/_{2}$ teaspoons vanilla extract
1 cup butter or margarine, softened
2 cups sugar
3 eggs
$3/4$ cup chocolate syrup
$1/4$ teaspoon baking soda
$1/4$ teaspoon peppermint extract (optional)

Grease the bottom of a 10-inch tube pan. Sift the flour, baking powder and salt together. Mix the milk and vanilla in a bowl.

Beat the butter in a mixer bowl until creamy. Add the sugar gradually, beating at high speed until light and fluffy. Beat in the eggs 1 at a time. Beat in the dry ingredients alternately with the milk mixture at low speed, beginning and ending with the dry ingredients.

Spoon $2/3$ of the batter into the prepared pan. Mix the remaining batter with the chocolate syrup, baking soda and flavoring in a bowl. Spoon over the prepared layer. Do not mix; the chocolate will end up in the center.

Bake at 350 degrees for 65 to 70 minutes or until the cake springs back when lightly touched in the center. Cool in pan on a wire rack. Remove to a serving plate; do not invert. Spread with your favorite frosting if desired.

Serves sixteen

Superb Pound Cake

3 cups flour
1/2 teaspoon baking powder
1/4 teaspoon salt
3 cups sugar
2 cups butter, softened
6 eggs, at room temperature
1 tablespoon lemon extract
1 tablespoon vanilla extract
1 cup milk

Sift the flour, baking powder and salt together. Cream the sugar and butter at medium speed in a mixer bowl until light and fluffy, scraping the bowl occasionally. Beat in the eggs 1 at a time. Stir in the flavorings.

Add the dry ingredients 1/3 cup at a time, mixing well after each addition. Beat in the milk just until blended. Spoon the batter into a greased and floured 10-inch tube pan.

Place the cake in a cold oven. Bake at 325 degrees for 1 1/4 hours or until a wooden pick inserted in the center comes out clean. Cool in the pan on a wire rack for 10 to 15 minutes. Remove to a wire rack to cool completely.

Serves sixteen

New Orleans Seven-Up Cake

1½ cups butter, softened
3 cups sugar
5 eggs, at room temperature
3 cups cake flour, sifted twice
3 tablespoons lemon extract
¾ cup Seven-Up, at room temperature

Coat the bottom and side of a bundt pan with shortening; dust lightly with cake flour.

Cream the butter by hand in a bowl for several minutes. Add the sugar 1 cup at a time, beating well after each addition until creamy. Beat in the eggs 1 at a time.

Fold in the cake flour 1 cup at a time. Add the flavoring and Seven-Up, beating just until blended. Spoon into the prepared pan.

Place the bundt pan on the middle oven rack. Bake at 325 degrees for 1½ hours or until a wooden pick inserted in the center comes out clean. Cool in the pan on a wire rack. Invert onto a cake plate.

Serves sixteen

Oatmeal Cake

1¼ cups boiling water
1 cup rolled oats
1⅓ cups flour
1 teaspoon baking soda
½ teaspoon salt
½ teaspoon cinnamon
1 cup packed brown sugar
1 cup sugar
½ cup margarine, softened
2 eggs
¾ cup packed brown sugar
½ cup margarine, softened
¼ cup evaporated milk
1 teaspoon vanilla extract
1 cup chopped nuts
1 cup shredded coconut

Mix the boiling water and oats in a bowl. Let stand for 20 minutes. Sift the flour, baking soda, salt and cinnamon together.

Beat 1 cup brown sugar, sugar, ½ cup margarine and eggs in a mixer bowl until smooth, scraping the bowl occasionally. Add the dry ingredients and mix well. Stir in the oat mixture.

Spoon into a greased and floured 9x13-inch cake pan. Bake at 350 degrees for 35 to 40 minutes or until the cake tests done.

Beat ¾ cup brown sugar, ½ cup margarine, evaporated milk and vanilla in a mixer bowl until blended. Stir in the nuts and coconut. Spread over the hot cake. Broil for 2 minutes or until light brown.

Serves fifteen

Deep-Dish Apple Pie

4 cups flour
2 teaspoons salt
2 teaspoons sugar
1 cup butter, chopped, chilled
3/4 cup nonfat sour cream
4 teaspoons ice water
15 large Granny Smith and/or McIntosh apples, sliced
lemon juice
3/4 cup sugar
1/2 cup packed brown sugar
1 (4-ounce) package vanilla instant pudding mix
2 teaspoons cinnamon
2 teaspoons nutmeg
1 teaspoon lemon zest
1/2 teaspoon salt
1 tablespoon low-fat margarine
milk
sugar to taste

Sift the flour, 2 teaspoons salt and 2 teaspoons sugar into a bowl and mix well. Cut in the butter until crumbly. Stir in the sour cream. Add the ice water gradually, stirring until a ball forms.

Knead gently 2 or 3 times. Shape into a ball and place in a sealable plastic bag. Chill for 2 hours.

Roll the dough into two rectangles on a lightly floured surface. Fit 1 rectangle into a 9 x 11-inch baking dish.

Sprinkle the apples with lemon juice in a bowl. Combine 3/4 cup sugar, brown sugar, pudding mix, cinnamon, nutmeg, lemon zest and 1/2 teaspoon salt in a bowl and mix well. Add the apples, tossing to coat. Spoon the apple mixture into the prepared dish. Dot with the margarine.

Top with the remaining pastry, fluting the edges and cutting vents. Brush the pastry with milk and sprinkle with sugar to taste. Bake at 375 degrees for 45 to 60 minutes or until golden brown and bubbly.

Serves six

Peach Pie

3 cups flour
1 teaspoon salt
1 cup shortening
6 tablespoons ice water
1 1/2 to 2 cups sugar
3 tablespoons flour
1/2 teaspoon cinnamon
1/4 teaspoon salt
1/4 teaspoon nutmeg
6 cups sliced fresh peaches
1 cup whipping cream
1/4 to 1/2 cup butter

Sift 3 cups flour and 1 teaspoon salt into a bowl and mix well. Reserve 1/4 cup of the mixture. Cut the shortening into the remaining flour mixture until crumbly.

Mix the reserved flour mixture and ice water to a paste in a bowl. Add to the crumb mixture, stirring to form a ball.

Divide the dough into 2 portions. Roll each portion into a 12-inch circle between sheets of waxed paper. Fit 1 pastry into a 9-inch pie plate.

Combine the sugar, 3 tablespoons flour, cinnamon, 1/4 teaspoon salt and nutmeg in a bowl and mix well. Add the peaches, tossing to coat. Spoon the peach mixture into the prepared pie plate. Pour the cream over the top. Dot with the butter.

Top with the remaining pastry, fluting the edge and cutting vents. Bake at 450 degrees for 15 minutes. Reduce the oven temperature to 350 degrees. Bake until brown and bubbly.

Serves six

Rum and Chocolate Pecan Pie

1¼ cups dark corn syrup
1 cup sugar
4 eggs
1 cup semisweet chocolate chips
¼ cup melted butter
2 tablespoons dark rum
1 teaspoon vanilla extract
2 to 3 cups broken pecans
Pie Pastry
pecan halves

Bring the corn syrup and sugar to a boil in a saucepan. Boil just until the sugar dissolves, stirring constantly. Cool slightly.

Whisk the eggs in a bowl until blended. Add the corn syrup mixture and chocolate chips gradually, stirring constantly until mixed. Stir in the butter, rum and vanilla. Add the broken pecans and mix well.

Spoon into the pastry-lined pie plate. Line the edge of the pie with pecan halves to form a border. Bake at 350 degrees for 50 to 60 minutes or until set.

Pie Pastry

1½ cups flour
¼ teaspoon salt
⅓ cup shortening, lard or butter, chilled
¼ cup ice water

Mix the flour and salt in a bowl. Cut in the shortening until blended and the mixture holds together when pinched. Add the ice water, mixing until the mixture forms a ball.

Roll the dough into a 12-inch circle on a lightly floured surface. Fit into a pie plate, trimming the overhang and crimping the edge. Freeze for 15 minutes or chill, covered with plastic wrap, for up to 24 hours.

Serves six

Pineapple Crumb Dessert

1 (20-ounce) can crushed pineapple
1 (14-ounce) can sweetened condensed milk
1 (14-ounce) package graham crackers, crushed
1/2 cup butter, softened

Drain most of the juice from the pineapple. Combine the pineapple and condensed milk in a bowl and mix well.

Mix the crushed graham crackers and butter in a bowl. Pat enough of the crumb mixture to measure 1/2 inch thick in a 9x9-inch baking dish. Layer the pineapple mixture and remaining crumb mixture 1/2 at a time in the prepared pan.

Bake at 375 degrees until heated through. Cool in the pan on a wire rack. Cut into squares.

Makes two dozen squares

Nobody can do everything, but everybody can do something, and if everybody does something, everything will get done. —Gil Scott-Heron

Our task is to make ourselves architects of the future.
—Jomo Mzee Kenyatta

The toughness of the wawa tree symbolizes human potential and the ability to achieve one's purpose. It suggests that the individual and the traits he exhibits are the true basis of nationhood and empowerment.

As we reach for empowerment, we become aware of the strength afforded by healthy lifestyles and the welcome knowledge that we do not have to give up the foods that nourish our spirits. Recipes in this section have been adjusted to reduce the fat content without loss of taste.

The Future
The Struggle for Low-Fat & Empowerment

WAWA ABA
(wah-wah ah-ba)

The seeds of the wawa tree

WAWA ABA is the symbol of hardiness, toughness, and perseverance.

Turkey Ham Salad Spread

1 cup minced turkey ham
2 sweet pickles, chopped
2 tablespoons minced onion
1 teaspoon freshly cracked pepper
1/4 cup nonfat mayonnaise-style salad dressing

Combine the turkey ham, pickles, onion and pepper in a bowl. Add the salad dressing and mix gently. Serve as an appetizer with crackers.

Serves four

Minted Tuna Spread

1 (8-ounce) can tuna, drained, flaked   *North Africa*
4 teaspoons vegetable oil
1 1/2 teaspoons chopped fresh mint
1/2 teaspoon nutmeg
1/2 teaspoon (or more) lemon juice

Combine the tuna, oil, mint, nutmeg and lemon juice in a bowl and mix well. Chill until serving time. Serve on bread points or in endive leaves.
For a luncheon dish, add dried beans cooked with chile pepper and spinach steamed in chicken or beef bouillon and drained.

Serves four

Nutritional information is for the basic spread only.

Fruit and Cheese Salad Ring

sections of 1 small orange   *Caribbean*
1 medium banana, chopped
1/2 cup juice-pack pineapple chunks, drained
2 envelopes unflavored gelatin
2 cups water
2 teaspoons orange extract
1 teaspoon coconut extract
2 or 3 drops yellow food coloring
1 1/3 cups cottage cheese

Combine the orange sections, banana and pineapple in a bowl and mix gently. Spoon into a ring mold.

Sprinkle the gelatin over 1 cup of the water in a saucepan and let stand to soften. Cook over low heat until the gelatin dissolves completely, stirring constantly. Remove from the heat.

Stir in the remaining 1 cup water, flavorings and food coloring. Spoon over the fruit in the ring mold. Chill until firm.

Unmold onto a lettuce-lined serving plate. Fill the center with the cottage cheese. Garnish with mint sprigs.

Substitute 1/2 cup juice-pack mandarin oranges for the fresh orange if desired.

Serves four

Potato Salad

4 pounds red potatoes with skins, scrubbed
3 ribs celery, chopped
1 small onion, finely chopped
2 medium carrots, grated
4 sweet pickles
4 hard-cooked egg whites
1 teaspoon seasoned salt
$1/2$ teaspoon pepper
3 tablespoons nonfat mayonnaise
3 tablespoons nonfat sour cream
1 teaspoon mustard
$1/4$ teaspoon paprika

Cook the potatoes in water in a saucepan for 15 to 20 minutes or until tender; drain. Cool and chop the potatoes.

Combine the potatoes, celery, onion, carrots, pickles, egg whites, salt and pepper in a bowl. Add the mayonnaise, sour cream and mustard and mix gently. Sprinkle with the paprika. Chill until serving time.

Serves eight

Baked Ham with Piquant Orange Sauce

1 (4-pound) smoked ham   *Haiti*
whole cloves
brown sugar substitute equal to ¹/₂ cup
    brown sugar
1 (6-ounce) can frozen orange juice
    concentrate, thawed
6 ounces onions, sliced
2 garlic cloves, minced
2 tablespoons water
2 packets instant beef broth and seasoning mix
3 cups water
¹/₄ cup tomato paste
2 teaspoons prepared mustard
1 teaspoon dehydrated orange peel

Score the ham diagonally into diamond shapes. Stud it with cloves and sprinkle with brown sugar substitute. Place on a rack in a baking pan. Bake at 325 degrees for 15 to 18 minutes per pound, basting with the orange juice concentrate.

Combine the onions, garlic, 2 tablespoons water and beef broth in a large nonstick skillet. Cook until the onions are light brown. Stir in 3 cups water and the tomato paste. Cook until reduced by ¹/₃ or until of the desired consistency. Stir in the mustard and orange peel.

Slice the ham and serve with the sauce.

Serves twelve

Chili Con Carne

1 pound dried kidney beans
1 tablespoon instant beef bouillon
12 ounces shredded roasted pork
1 medium green bell pepper, chopped
3/4 cup tomato purée
2 garlic cloves, crushed
1 tablespoon onion flakes
1 teaspoon chili powder
1/2 teaspoon oregano
1/8 teaspoon ground cumin
4 medium canned tomatoes

Pick the beans and rinse well. Combine with water to cover in a saucepan and bring to a boil. Cook until tender, adding additional water as needed. Drain the beans, reserving 1 cup of the liquid. Dissolve the beef bouillon in the reserved liquid.

Combine the beans, pork, beef bouillon mixture, green pepper, tomato purée, garlic, onion flakes, chili powder, oregano and cumin in a large saucepan.

Add the tomatoes, crushing against the sacepan with a wooden spoon. Simmer for 40 minutes or until of the desired consistency.

Vary the dish by adding 1/4 teaspoon chocolate extract, omitting the tomatoes, substituting beef for the pork or pinto beans for the kidney, or adding peppers.

Serves six

Chicken Curry

6 ounces onions, finely chopped   Trinidad
2 cups chicken bouillon
2 garlic cloves, crushed
1½ tablespoons Caribbean Curry Powder, or to taste
2¼ pounds chopped cooked chicken or turkey
6 ounces Hubbard squash, peeled, sliced
3 cups sliced peeled eggplant
3 cups sliced peeled chayote
1 hot chile pepper, seeded, chopped, or to taste
1 teaspoon lime juice
½ teaspoon salt

Cook the onions in a small amount of the chicken bouillon in a saucepan until golden brown. Add the garlic and curry powder and cook for 3 to 4 minutes, stirring constantly.

Add the remaining chicken bouillon, chicken, squash, eggplant, chayote and chile pepper. Simmer, covered, until the vegetables are tender. Stir in the lime juice and salt.

Substitute West Indian pumpkin for the squash when available.

Serves six

Caribbean Curry Powder

2 tablespoons cumin seeds
1 tablespoon each coriander seeds, poppy seeds, brown
     mustard seeds, whole cloves and peppercorns
2 tablespoons ground turmeric
1 tablespoon ground Jamaican ginger

Toast the cumin seeds, coriander seeds, poppy seeds and mustard seeds in a cast-iron skillet until the mustard seeds begin to jump. Combine with the cloves and peppercorns in a blender or mortar and process until ground. Mix in the turmeric and ginger. Sift into an airtight container.

Makes ten tablespoons

Fetri Detsi
Chicken and Okra

4 (6-ounce) boneless skinless chicken breasts   *Congo*
1 teaspoon salt
2 medium tomatoes, peeled, finely chopped
3 hot green chiles, seeded, finely chopped
4 ounces onion, chopped
1 (2-inch) piece fresh ginger, finely chopped
4 cups water
12 ounces fresh or frozen okra, sliced
¼ cup tomato paste
2 cups cooked rice

Sprinkle the chicken with the salt. Combine with the tomatoes, chiles, onion and ginger in a heavy saucepan. Add the water. Bring to a boil and reduce the heat. Simmer, covered for 20 minutes.

Add the okra and tomato paste. Simmer, uncovered, until the chicken and vegetables are tender.

Arrange the chicken over the rice on serving plates. Spoon the vegetables and sauce over the chicken.

Serves four

The key word, though, is planning; good health doesn't just happen. You have to make it happen.
—Victoria Johnson, author

Arroz con Pollo
Chicken with Rice

1 (8-ounce) boneless chicken breast
2 ounces onion, finely chopped
1/4 cup sliced mushrooms
1/2 medium tomato, peeled, chopped
1 ounce cooked peas
1/2 cup cooked rice
1 tablespoon chopped pimento
1/2 cup tomato juice
1/2 cup chicken bouillon
1/2 teaspoon salt
1/4 teaspoon pepper

Caribbean

Place the chicken on a rack in a broiler pan. Broil 4 inches from the heat source for 8 to 10 minutes or until brown, turning frequently. Cut the chicken into bite-size pieces, discarding the skin.

Cook the onion and mushrooms in a nonstick skillet sprayed with nonfat cooking spray until light brown. Combine with the chicken, tomato, peas, rice and pimento in a small baking dish.

Stir in the tomato juice and chicken bouillon. Season with the salt and pepper. Bake, covered, at 375 degrees for 15 to 20 minutes or until the liquid is absorbed.

Serves one

Fish Stew

Caribbean

4 cups coarsely chopped spinach
12 ounces fresh or frozen okra, sliced
1/2 cup finely chopped celery
3 cups water
3/4 cup tomato purée
1/2 small hot red pepper (optional)
1/4 teaspoon thyme
1/2 bay leaf
salt and black pepper to taste
1 1/2 pounds fish fillets, cut into 1-inch pieces

Combine the spinach, okra, celery and water in a saucepan. Bring to a boil and cook for 6 minutes.

Stir in the tomato purée, red pepper, thyme, bay leaf, salt and black pepper. Place the fish on top. Bring to a boil and reduce the heat.

Simmer for 10 minutes or until the fish flakes easily, spooning the liquid over the fish several times. Discard the bay leaf to serve.

Substitute turnip greens for the spinach or canned okra for the fresh or frozen okra, adding it with the tomato purée.

Serves four

Jambalaya

1 pound boneless skinless chicken breasts, cut into strips
1 pound turkey sausage, chopped
2 pounds peeled shrimp
3 teaspoons olive oil
5 garlic cloves, minced
½ cup chopped onion
2 carrots, finely chopped
1 each red and green bell pepper, seeded, chopped
¼ cup chopped scallions
4 tomatoes, peeled, chopped
¼ cup minced parsley
8 basil leaves, minced
2 bay leaves
1 cup reduced-calorie beer
¼ cup tomato paste
2 tablespoons Worcestershire sauce
1 teaspoon each thyme and ground ginger
1½ teaspoons seasoned salt
¼ teaspoon cayenne pepper
1 teaspoon black pepper
3 cups nonfat chicken stock
1 cup uncooked long grain rice

Sauté the chicken, sausage and shrimp in 1 teaspoon of the olive oil in a saucepan until the shrimp turn pink. Remove the chicken, sausage and shrimp from the saucepan. Add the remaining 2 teaspoons olive oil and the garlic to the saucepan. Sauté for 1 minute. Add the onion, carrots, bell peppers and scallions. Sauté just until tender-crisp.

Stir in the tomatoes, parsley, basil and bay leaves. Simmer for 20 minutes, stirring frequently. Add the next 8 ingredients and 1 cup of the stock. Simmer for 20 minutes or until thickened.

Add the remaining 2 cups stock and bring to a boil. Stir in the rice. Simmer, covered, for 15 minutes or until the rice is tender. Add the chicken, sausage and shrimp. Cook for 10 minutes longer. Let stand for 15 minutes before serving. Discard the bay leaves.

Serves eight

Portuguese Shrimp

6 ounces large shrimp, peeled, deveined
1 teaspoon sauterne or sherry extract
1/4 teaspoon minced fresh gingerroot
1/4 teaspoon salt
black pepper to taste
1/2 cup tomato purée
1 teaspoon Worcestershire sauce
1/2 medium green bell pepper, chopped
1/2 medium red bell pepper, chopped
1 ounce scallions, sliced
1 tablespoon onion flakes
1 teaspoon chopped fennel leaves, or
    several drops of anise extract

Season the shrimp with the sauterne extract, gingerroot, salt and black pepper. Let stand for 20 minutes.

Combine the shrimp with the tomato purée, Worcestershire sauce, bell peppers, scallions, onion flakes and fennel leaves in a saucepan. Simmer, covered, for 10 minutes or just until the shrimp turn pink; do not overcook.

Serves one

Crowder Peas

2 pounds dried crowder peas
1 cup low-sodium smoked turkey ham, chopped
1 cup chopped onion
1 tablespoon chopped garlic
1/4 cup chopped green bell pepper
2 low-sodium beef bouillon cubes
1 teaspoon Mrs. Dash® original seasoning
1 teaspoon salt substitute
1/2 teaspoon pepper

Pick and rinse the peas. Combine with water to cover in a saucepan and let stand overnight; drain.

Combine the peas with the turkey ham, onion, garlic, green pepper, bouillon cubes, Mrs. Dash® seasoning, salt substitute, black pepper and enough water to just cover in a saucepan. Cook for 45 minutes or until the peas are tender but still firm, adding additional water if necessary.

Serves twelve

The food we eat can be either our poison or our medicine.
—Queen Afua, author

Garlic Mashed Potatoes

2 (8-ounce) potatoes
2 large garlic cloves, chopped
1/2 cup skim milk
1/2 teaspoon white pepper

Peel the potatoes and cut into quarters. Cook, covered, in a small amount of water in a saucepan for 20 to 25 minutes or until tender. Drain, reserving the potatoes in the covered saucepan.

Cook the garlic in the skim milk in a saucepan for 30 minutes or until the garlic is tender. Add to the potatoes with the white pepper. Beat at low speed with a mixer or mash with a potato masher until smooth.

To prepare in the microwave, prick the unpeeled potatoes with a fork and place on a microwave-safe plate. Microwave on High for 12 minutes or until tender, turning once. Let stand for 5 minutes. Combine the milk and garlic in a 4-cup glass measure. Microwave on Medium for 4 minutes or until the garlic is tender. Peel the potatoes and cut into quarters. Combine and mash as above.

Serves four

It's better to look ahead and prepare than to look back and regret. —Jackie Joyner-Kersee,
American Olympic athlete

Turnip and Mustard Greens

2 pounds turnip greens
2 pounds mustard greens
5 cups water
1 pound lean smoked turkey, chopped
1 medium onion, chopped
2 low-sodium chicken bouillon cubes
1 tablespoon Mrs. Dash® original seasoning
1 teaspoon sugar
1 teaspoon lemon pepper

Wash the greens well, discarding the stems and shaking off excess water. Gather into small bunches and cut into smaller pieces.

Bring the water to a boil in a large saucepan. Add the greens to the water and bring to a simmer. Add the turkey, onion, bouillon, Mrs. Dash® seasoning, sugar and lemon pepper.

Simmer, covered, for 1 hour or until the greens are tender. Adjust the seasonings before serving.

Serves twelve

New Orleans Red Beans *Good*

1 pound dried red beans
2 quarts water
1½ cups chopped onions
1 cup chopped celery
4 bay leaves
1 cup chopped green bell pepper
3 tablespoons chopped garlic
3 tablespoons chopped parsley
2 teaspoons crushed dried thyme
1 teaspoon salt
1 teaspoon black pepper

Pick and rinse the beans. Combine with the water, onions, celery and bay leaves in a 5-quart saucepan. Bring to a boil and reduce the heat.

Simmer, covered, for 1½ hours or until the beans are tender, stirring occasionally. Mash some of the beans against the side of the saucepan.

Add the green pepper, garlic, parsley, thyme, salt and black pepper. Simmer, uncovered, for 30 minutes longer or until of the desired consistency.

Discard the bay leaves and serve over cooked brown rice.

Serves eight

Nutritional information does not include the rice.

Coconut Rice and Beans Ochos Rios

4 ounces onion, chopped *Jamaica*
¾ cup chicken bouillon
½ hot red chile pepper
⅛ teaspoon thyme
⅛ teaspoon salt
1 cup cooked rice
12 ounces cooked dried kidney beans
2 tablespoons evaporated skim milk
½ teaspoon coconut extract

Cook the onion in a nonstick saucepan over high heat until brown, stirring constantly. Add the chicken bouillon, chile pepper, thyme and salt and bring to a boil.

Stir in the rice and beans and reduce the heat. Simmer for 20 minutes or until the liquid is absorbed. Stir in the evaporated milk and coconut extract. Cook just until heated through.

For a main dish, reduce the beans to 8 ounces and add 6 ounces of cooked pork.

Serves two

The day on which one starts out is not the time to start one's preparations. —Nigerian proverb

Feijão com Arroz
Black Beans and Rice

1 medium green bell pepper, chopped   Brazil
1 small garlic clove, crushed
1/2 teaspoon oregano
1/4 teaspoon ground cumin
1/4 cup beef bouillon
8 ounces cooked dried black beans
1/2 cup cooked brown rice
1 slice red onion

Combine the green pepper, garlic, oregano, cumin and beef bouillon in a saucepan. Simmer for 10 minutes.

Stir in the beans and rice. Simmer until heated through. Ladle into bowls and serve with the onion slice.

Serves one

The cultural [historic] memory is ceaselessly renewed retroactively by new discoveries. Our past by continually modifying itself through our discoveries, invites us to new appropriations; these appropriations lead us toward a better grasp of our identity. —Okonda Okolo, philosopher

Grits with Vegetables

24 ounces cooked dried chick-peas
3 cups sliced zucchini
3 cups sliced Swiss chard
2 cups coarsely chopped carrots
2 cups coarsely chopped turnips
6 ounces onions, sliced
6 ribs celery, chopped
6 sprigs of parsley
1/8 teaspoon turmeric
1/8 teaspoon red pepper
1 cup beef bouillon
1/4 to 1/2 teaspoon cinnamon
1/4 teaspoon whole cloves
4 1/2 cups cooked hominy grits

Combine the chick-peas, zucchini, Swiss chard, carrots, turnips, onions, celery, parsley, turmeric and red pepper in a steamer or heavy saucepan. Add the beef bouillon and enough water to just cover the vegetables.

Stir the cinnamon and cloves into the grits. Place in the top of the steamer or in a colander lined with cheesecloth in the top of the saucepan. Cover the steamer or saucepan, lining with additional cheesecloth if necessary to ensure a tight seal.

Steam for 30 minutes or until the vegetables are tender and the grits have absorbed the flavors. Mound the grits and vegetables on a platter to serve.

Substitute cabbage for the Swiss chard or add 12 ounces of cooked frankfurters to the chick-pea mixture if desired.

Serves six

Corn Bread Surprise

2 cups yellow cornmeal
1 cup flour
1½ tablespoons baking powder
2 tablespoons dark brown sugar
1½ teaspoons salt
3 eggs
1⅓ cups 1% milk
½ cup melted reduced-fat margarine
1 cup whole kernel corn
½ cup shredded Cheddar cheese
½ cup grated carrot
½ cup grated onion
¼ cup minced jalapeño peppers

Mix the cornmeal, flour, baking powder, brown sugar and salt in a large bowl. Combine the eggs, milk and margarine in a medium bowl and beat until smooth. Stir into the cornmeal mixture. Add the corn, cheese, carrot, onion and peppers and mix well.

Spoon into greased muffin cups. Bake at 400 degrees until a wooden pick inserted into the muffins comes out clean.

Makes twenty-four muffins

Old-Fashioned Bread Pudding

10 slices whole wheat bread
1 egg
3 egg whites
1½ cups skim milk
¼ cup sugar
¼ cup packed brown sugar
1 teaspoon vanilla extract
½ teaspoon cinnamon
¼ teaspoon nutmeg
¼ teaspoon ground cloves
2 teaspoons sugar

Spray an 8x8-inch baking dish with nonstick vegetable spray and arrange the bread in 2 rows, overlapping to fit.

Combine the egg, egg whites, skim milk, ¼ cup sugar, brown sugar and vanilla in a bowl and beat until smooth. Pour over the bread.

Mix the cinnamon, nutmeg, cloves and 2 teaspoons sugar in a small bowl. Sprinkle the mixture over the bread.

Bake at 350 degrees for 30 to 35 minutes or until the top is brown and firm. Serve warm or at room temperature.

Serves nine

Nutritional Information

Persons with dietary or health problems or whose diets require close monitoring should not rely solely on the nutritional information provided. They should consult their physician or a registered dietitian for specific information.

Abbreviations for Nutritional Profile

Cal — Calories
Prot — Protein
Carbo — Carbohydrates

T Fat — Total Fat
Chol — Cholesterol
Fiber — Dietary Fiber

Sod — Sodium
g — grams
mg — milligrams

- The nutritional profile is based on all measurements being level.
- Chicken, cooked for boning and chopping, has been roasted to yield the lowest caloric values.
- Cottage cheese is cream-style with 4.2% creaming mixture.
- Eggs are all large.
- Flour is unsifted all-purpose flour.
- Garnishes, serving suggestions, and other optional additions and variations are not included.
- Margarine and butter are regular, not whipped or presoftened.
- Salt and other ingredients to taste as noted in the ingredients have not been included.
- If a choice of ingredients has been given, the profile reflects the first option. If a choice of amounts has been given, the profile reflects the greater amount.

Pg #	Recipe Title (Approx Per Serving)	Cal	Prot (g)	Carbo (g)	T Fat (g)	% Cal from Fat	Chol (mg)	Fiber (g)	Sod (mg)
150	Turkey Ham Salad Spread	107	7	11	4	33	31	<1	751
150	Minted Tuna Spread	106	14	<1	5	44	17	0	192
151	Fruit and Cheese Salad Ring	146	13	18	3	20	10	2	292
152	Potato Salad	253	7	57	<1	1	0	6	412
153	Baked Ham with Piquant Orange Sauce	190	28	9	5	22	74	1	2083
154	Chili con Carne	406	30	50	11	23	35	13	1348
155	Chicken Curry	347	45	13	12	33	128	5	824
155	Caribbean Curry Powder	24	1	3	1	39	0	1	5
156	Fetri Detsi (Chicken and Okra)	369	40	41	5	12	94	5	809
157	Arroz con Pollo (Chicken with Rice)	443	53	42	7	14	125	5	2463
158	Fish Stew	197	32	13	2	10	80	5	354
159	Jambalaya	368	40	30	9	22	214	3	813
160	Portuguese Shrimp	212	26	26	2	7	202	6	1407
161	Crowder Peas	244	17	41	2	7	8	12	108
162	Garlic Mashed Potatoes	100	3	22	<1	1	1	2	21
163	Turnip and Mustard Greens	76	10	9	1	12	16	5	422
164	New Orleans Red Beans	197	14	37	<1	1	0	14	312
165	Coconut Rice and Beans Ochos Rios	365	19	69	2	4	1	12	727
166	Feijão com Arroz (Black Beans and Rice)	456	24	87	2	5	0	24	300
167	Grits with Vegetables	358	15	68	4	9	0	13	355
168	Corn Bread Surprise	112	4	16	4	31	30	1	318
169	Old-Fashioned Bread Pudding	153	6	29	2	11	24	2	213

Of the People: An African American Cooking Experience

Mail Order Department
Charles H. Wright Museum of African American History
315 East Warren Avenue
Detroit, Michigan 48201

Qty	Your Order	Total
_____	*Of the People: An African American Cooking Experience* at $21.95 each	$ _____
	Michigan residents add 6% sales tax	$ _____
_____	Postage and handling at $6.00 each	$ _____
	Total	$ _____

Name
_____

Street Address
_____

City _____ State _____ Zip _____

Telephone
_____

Method of Payment: [   ] VISA   [   ] MasterCard   [   ] American Express

[   ] Check payable to Charles H. Wright Museum of African
American History

Account Number _____ Expiration Date _____

Signature
_____

Join the Charles H. Wright Museum of African American History.

Benefits include personalized membership card, free admission to the Exhibition Galleries, subscription to the quarterly newsletter, 10% discount on Museum Store purchases, and notices of events and programs. Membership charges are $15 for college students and senior citizens, $35 for an individual, $55 for a family, and $100 for a contributor. For information call 313-494-5800 and ask for the Membership Office.

Photocopies will be accepted.